PETER "SUGARFOOT" CUNNINGHAM'S

CIVILIZED WARRING

Fundamental Kickboxing Techniques

AS TOLD TO
ROBERT "SNAKE" MICKEY

Edited by Lisa Hanks

Designed by Greg Compton

Photography by Craig Incardone

Peter Cunningham is assisted by Robert Mickey

Shot at the Outlaw Boxing Gym, Hollywood, California

Printed in the United States of America

ISBN 0-9649331-0-1

Published by:

Ragnar's
B♦O♦O♦K♦S
A DIVISION OF
GALT PUBLISHING

800/400-0890

Neither the authors nor the publisher assumes any responsibility for the use or
misuse of the information contained in this book; it is intended for
entertainment purposes only.
If the reader practices any of the techniques in this book, he does so at his own
risk. Any injuries that may result from such acts are solely the responsibility of the
reader. These techniques should be practiced and studied only under the guidance
of a qualified instructor. Before beginning any type of physical exercise, including
those contained in this book, the reader should consult a physician.

TABLE OF CONTENTS

FOREWORD

While teaching at a seminar in Canada, in which a wide variety of styles were presented to enthusiastic martial arts aspirants, there was, among the various sensei who were sharing their accumulated knowledge with numerous attendees, a muscular, gentlemanly young man. His dynamic techniques, expert use of the training equipment and willingness to answer every question with patience and clarity, made the younger participants feel at ease and greatly impressed those who were "old hands" as seminar attendees.

That was kickboxing champ Peter "Sugarfoot" Cunningham.

With a record that is unblemished as of this writing, I salute him as one of the truly great young stars in the martial arts world. And I am extremely pleased and proud that he asked me to write this foreword.

Comparable to the likes of Michael Jordan in fluidity, speed and kinesiological control, Peter teaches utilization of combinations, distancing, evasiveness and his fabulous kicking techniques. It quickly becomes apparent that as incredible as his moves are, his teaching skills are such that those whom he instructs always come away feeling that they, too, can eventually learn and perfect the techniques they were taught. This singular quality separates the true sensei from the mere exhibitionist: the ability to impart knowledge and instill confidence in those who place their trust in a teacher, over and above the prosaic showing of one's skills, however evolved said skills may be. This book covers such subjects as: choosing a school, choosing and correctly using equipment and fully absorbing the concepts and strategies of new techniques.

Cunningham equates kickboxing with the game of life. Indeed, he has made it his way of life; a fact that can be attested to by others in his community. This is something I can definitely relate to, having been born into a prominent martial arts family upon whom my own friends, neighbors and local Board of Education look to for aid and leadership on a day-to-day basis. His philosophy and opinions regarding how you may look within your Art to find the answer to a host of challenges, be they physical, social or emotional, that you encounter during your life is another thing that you will find throughout this truly great book.

In reading this book, you will be receiving instruction from a man who is most definitely on a comparable level with the likes of such living legends as Joe Lewis, Benny "the Jet" Urquidez and Bill "Superfoot" Wallace, as well as other great names in martial arts history.

Prepare to be educated in a new and unique manner that will definitely add to your repertoire of techniques. You're guaranteed a good read.

Michael DePasquale, Jr.
Publisher/Editor Karate International *magazine*
Ni-Dai Shihan, Yoshitsune Jujitsu
Founder, Federation of United Martial Artists

INTRODUCTION

W hen I was a little kid, I spent a lot of time watching Bruce Lee movies, thinking, "Here's a little guy beating up all these big guys. I'm a little guy—I can do that." As it was, even as a bony little 9-year-old I was beating up older kids in the neighborhood. I would always kick and punch and use my feet, and some of the guys would say, "You girl, why you gotta kick?" But to me kicking was cool. I'd go to the Saturday matinees and see these Chinese guys kick somebody in the head or fly in the air and try to kick somebody, and I'd think, "Yeah, that's cool. I'm going to be a fighter one day."

For me, kickboxing has been the ultimate. It's given me an arena to satisfy my desire to be the absolute best at what I do, to be legendary in my sport. That may be what it has to offer to you, too, but it doesn't have to be. Kickboxing has appeal for just about everyone. Whether you're looking for a full-contact sport to challenge your athleticism, a demanding physical workout or a very effective method of self-defense for the real world, kickboxing fits the bill.

As we move from technique to technique, I'll address how they apply to the various interests of each of you. If you're a young dragon chomping to get into the ring, you'll learn a lot. And you won't just learn dry technique. You'll benefit from my personal experiences over 18 years of training, and what it's told me about what works, what doesn't and when you should try it. Since I'm a professional fighter, my perspective is from inside the ring.

But as a teacher, I've also trained the suburban mother who wants to learn a few effective self-defense moves so she can walk in public with a little more confidence. You just need to promise me up front, Mom, that you won't use any of these moves on Dad or the kids. Deal?

Oh, and if you're just looking for a killer way to keep in shape, don't worry. Just following along and doing what we instruct will take care of that, no problem.

If you've had martial arts training in the past, a little or a lot, you may find it helpful in kickboxing, but it's not necessary. It's a bigger help if your goal is to fight professionally, as the discipline and self-control taught in most martial arts, as well as the diligence required to achieve the necessary kicking skills, are an absolute must. However, a drawback to the traditional route is the tendency to sometimes take control too far, to the point of not having any real power behind your strikes. So there are plusses and minusses.

I started out with traditional martial arts training, back when I was 14. A friend of mine, who was a 14-year-old brown belt, invited me to his karate school. I thought, "A brown belt, wow, that's neat, because after that comes black. Great!"

I think eventually I would have taken to martial arts anyway, but it just worked out so well the way it happened. So instead of waiting two, three years down the road and saying, "Mom, I'm a man now, and I'm gonna do my own stuff," it was, "Mom, will you take me there, please?"

So I went to my friend's karate school, and met his sensei, Robert Supeen. I found I could be serious, could be taught discipline, and I learned to move. I decided, "This is me."

I'd always had a burning desire to be the best, and I give Sensei Bob Supeen, Sr., and Sensei Bob Supeen, Jr., a lot of credit for pushing me in that direction. They worked their students very hard. We would work for a karate tournament, a point fight tournament, as though it were the Olympics. Seven days a week we were in the gym, training. Why? To win. To be the best.

Now, the very first tournament he took me to, my sensei said, "Come here. Heh, heh, heh. See these trophies?" I said, "Yeah," Third place. Second place. First place. He goes, "You're not concerned about these," pointing to the second and third place trophies. I said, "Yeah, I know the way you think." This is a man who brushed aside those at the tournaments who hadn't won.

Then he walked over to this special trophy, and pointed to it. "This one. What's it say, son."

I said, "Best Technician."

He goes, "That's the one you want. I've received two of these in my life. Competing all these years. Hard to get. But you don't worry about that one now."

That trophy was always awarded to a black belt. End of story, no question about it. So, when I became a black belt, then I would compete for it. I was an orange belt; it was my very first tournament.

The tournament started, and I'm fighting all these guys. The lightweight division is usually the biggest division—maybe 50 guys or so. We just narrowed it down. After the first fight, only half the guys were left. After four or five fights, I had whupped everybody.

Then it was announced, "Usually this trophy is awarded to a black belt who shows outstanding ability. This year we have a surprise. It goes to a young man from Bob Supeen's gym. Peter Cunningham."

"Wow," I think, "Can someone help me with my head?" I could feel it swelling by the minute. And then Sensei Bob turns to me and says, "Don't let it go to your head. When we get you back to the gym, you'll get your butt whipped by all the guys."

Bob kept me honest, but at the same time, he says, "You win, you always win." That, I think, was a very big part of me becoming a fighter.

A friend of mine, a very good fighter, Hector Lopez always says, "If some guy loses a fight everyone'll say, 'This guy's a real good loser. You have to be a good winner and a good loser.'" Then Hector adds, "No, man. Forget that. You show me a good loser and I'll show you a loser."

That's why I'm so proud of my undefeated record. I guess, in a way, it tells me in the back of my mind, I don't want to be a good loser.

I know. You're thinking, "There he goes again, just talking about fighting." But am I?

Winning and losing isn't just about fighting—it's about life. The drive to win, to be your best, isn't confined to the ring. It's what you live every day, and what you decide your life's going to be.

The legendary Benny "The Jet" Urquidez asked me one time, "What do you want, what are you aspiring for, what are you shooting for, Petey, in kickboxing? What would you like to be in this?"

I said, "Well, sir, I'd like to, um, I'd like to become as, ah, as good as you or Bill Wallace." I was speaking my heart, but I didn't want to sound too cocky.

He goes, "No, son. You want to be better."

And I said, "Yes."

He goes, "Yes, always better. Never settle."

And I said, "Yeah. That's what I want to do."

Now tell me, is that just kickboxing advice, or is that a way to live your life?

There are many similarities between kickboxing and life in general. Like the fact that success is usually a combination of a number of factors, and not one trait alone. I've seen some really, really talented fighters, guys who make me look bad, not succeed because they lack the work ethic it takes to be the best. Maybe they don't have the heart, or a big enough goal to shoot for. Talent goes a long way, but talent without drive, without inspiration, without hard work, is going to fall by the wayside.

Lady Luck often plays a role, too. I've seen fighters that are good, even great, get into their first or second match and, bap, something happens. A cut, a broken arm, maybe a detached retina—and that's it. The guy was great, but that's it.

I suppose I should say something about injuries up front. This sport *is* kickboxing. If you get to the sparring stage or beyond, you're going to get hit. Sometimes hard. Injuries will happen, it's part and parcel of the game. Often injuries are self-inflicted, such as sprained or broken knuckles or toes, and are caused by improper technique or inadequate preparation.

We'll go over the safeguards you can use to avoid injuries, such as the proper way to wrap your hands and what you should be looking for in protective equipment. Many injuries can be avoided by using common sense.

If you make it a point to be thinking at all times and always follow the safety precautions I recommend, you can avoid many of the silly, but painful injuries that can occur. Maybe Joe says, "We're just going to go easy today, so I'll keep these little gloves on." Whap. "Oops. Sorry." And suddenly your nose is bleeding or Joe's trying to figure out how he's going to use his computer with one hand, because he broke a knuckle using the wrong gloves.

Supervised sparring definitely keeps injuries down. In the workouts themselves, when you're punching and kicking air to learn the techniques, very few, if any injuries occur. But, when you're sparring with somebody, there's a human factor, usually adrenaline. Don't get excited. An instructor always has to keep everybody calm. But as a fighter, you have to say to yourself, "Okay, keep cool." Keep your head in the ring and you're more likely to win. And sharp instructors will keep injuries down by keeping the training situation in hand.

Of course, if you're going to be a professional, you're going to get popped hard, and eventually you're going to get hurt. I think the worst injury I've ever sustained in the ring was a cut under my left eye from a head butt. Three or four years ago, I was fighting Lafayette Lawson, at Caesar's Palace in Las Vegas. I threw a punch, and missed a punch. That's a tricky situation. A fighter's going to counterpunch you after that. I could weave from a punch, I could slip a punch, but I like doing little tricks with my hands to stop a punch—so I missed, whoops, but I put my hand on his head to stop him in his tracks.

Unfortunately, Lawson used Jheri curl; he had the long hair with the juice in it. I put my glove on it and my hand just slips off. As he pushes, I push him and, ahh, his head's in my face. Oh, no. I hated it. I made sure I made it clear to the commentator after the fight. "I've got one, two, three cuts on my face. It wasn't my mistake. It wasn't like somebody punched me and did that, alright? So, I hope the fans are listening because I always teach safety. Accidents will happen, you know."

Skill, training and conditioning go a long way to help prevent injuries. The rest is simply luck. But the name of the game in kickboxing is to be the one doing the hitting, not the one being hit. My style isn't so much the macho, let's-see-who-can-take-the-most-punishment approach, but the quick, get-in-and-get-out method that keeps me pretty. I hit you, but you don't hit me. In the course of the fight, you're going to get some in, but I'm going to give three or four to your one.

There's an art to winning a fight. It's not just a show of who's more macho. If you go that route, at the end of the fight your brains cave in, and maybe he's hit you one time extra so he wins the fight. Me, I go bang, bang, bang, and I'm gone again. Dancing, dancing, and I'll do my clowning, try to make him angry. Make him swing so maybe I can tag him again. Then ding, the last bell goes and I win the fight. He may be mad, but hey, like I said, there's an art to winning a fight.

Now, if we're talking about meeting somebody in a back alley with a pipe or something, that's different. But that attacker in the back alley probably doesn't have any martial arts training (or he wouldn't have the pipe), and he's not expecting you to either. So we'll talk about some quick, devastating moves that will make the thug with the pipe wish he'd made a better career decision.

One of the reasons kickboxing is so effective as a method of self-defense is the "reality" of kickboxing versus other martial arts. Style is important, yes, but you're using all of your natural weapons to their fullest extent. Well, almost all of your weapons, since it's hard to bite someone with your mouthpiece in, and it's severely frowned upon in the ring. But if you want to bite some mugger on the street, hey, it's your call.

I've always had this self-defense thing in the back of my mind. The world is getting rough. Things were always rough, depending on where you live. In your neighborhood, though it's good to be civilized, what if the other guy's got different ideas?

"Hey, give me your wallet."

"I wish I could throw a punch now," you think. "I wish I could bob and weave and dodge."

While I hope it doesn't happen to you, there's always that blue moon. The blue moon hits you, now what? A little preparation makes a big difference in self-defense. One properly executed maneuver can make you a victor instead of a victim. But you've got to make the effort ahead of time.

Preparation takes some time, and some training. Like anything worthwhile in life, kickboxing requires a certain amount of commitment to be effective. Your level of commitment will vary, depending on whether you're the dragon or the mom. How much you put into it is a personal decision you'll need to make when you begin your training, but no workout regimen will give you satisfactory results if you take an every-now-and-then approach, and it's even more important with kickboxing.

The kicks and punches you will learn are demanding, and if you're lackadaisical in your approach, you'll be liable to be sore, both from asking too much from unconditioned muscles and maybe taking a shot you should've stopped if you'd been sharp. As usual, dedication yields great dividends.

My workouts are crazy, because it's always a tug-of-war between the two coaches at the gym. One is a kickboxing instructor, and one's a boxing instructor, and they both want the good fighters in their classes to impress the other guys, keep them training and attract new students.

When I was younger, I'd go to the boxing gym. (Back then training and gyms weren't as consolidated as they are now.) The boxing instructors didn't know I had a karate workout afterwards. Their attitude was, "Forget that karate stuff. Forget that kickboxing stuff. You should just do boxing. You're good kid." Just do boxing.

And at the karate gym, they didn't care if I'd just finished my boxing workout. "Get on your *gi*. Get going." I did it and hoped they'd cut me some slack. But I didn't bet on it.

And they both tried to corner me, and ask me which I liked best, boxing or kickboxing. I'd always say, "I like fighting, sir." That way I'm the diplomat.

Ed Couzens was an old boxing coach of mine. Straight boxing. He always worked with me in my kickboxing fights. He's a specialist. If you're going to fight professionally, you should have someone who works only your hands as well as a kickboxing coach. But *you* have to put it together. Both of them are with you at your fights in your corner.

"Okay, you need more kicking. Two kicks here." Then the other guy says, "Now you put the jab in and follow it with the right hand." It may sound confusing, but it works, I promise you.

Of course, if you don't intend to fight professionally, two coaches won't be necessary. A good kickboxing gym will be more than sufficient to meet your training needs. A qualified instructor can assist you in all aspects of your workout, from conditioning through punching, kicking and defense.

Your goals should be the know-how, the skills and the abilities. There is no recognized belt system in kickboxing, although some schools have devised one because the Western mind tends to want something to grasp or shoot for. You can usually gauge a kickboxer by how long he's been training. Two years is a relative beginner, but it varies; some kids can be dynamite in three.

If your intent is not to step into the ring, then you'll be the best judge of your progress, if you're honest with yourself. You'll know how well you're performing the techniques by the way they look and feel, and if you're too far off, I'm sure your instructor will kindly let you know. We'll discuss how to select the kickboxing gym and instructor that's right for you a little later.

Also no kata, or forms, are practiced in kickboxing. Judo has kata, jujitsu, grappling, has kata. (You see a grappler on the floor rolling around, holding himself, twisting himself, practicing kata. "Excuse me, man, what are you doing?" "Practicing kata." "Get off the floor. Get out of the school.") In Tae Kwon Do and Karate, you can do kata. It helps with balance and technique.

What you do in kickboxing and boxing is shadowbox. Fighting an imaginary opponent, usually in front of the mirror. In some kata, you would go way beyond that. You would do the swan, taking flight. It's beautiful, but most kata are just okay. Me, I hit this guy, I attack him, I come back and hit this guy. I think my way's more fun.

I also think my way is more appealing to many individuals today. For the people who got involved with martial arts as part of the fitness craze of the last 10 or 20 years, physical fitness is their primary focus. Most hardcore fighters picture themselves as samurai or ninja. Boxers see themselves as maybe knights, or soldiers from medieval times. They see themselves as warriors.

This deep-rooted feeling, it's a calling from the past. Fighting is how they can live it. Running is pretty tough, sure. Or I suppose they could play soccer or baseball, but no, they want to box, they want to war. Kickboxing is civilized warring.

Often kickboxing doesn't even require a real opponent, just a heavy bag. A lot of guys come into the gym just to work out the frustrations of your basic day at the office. They say they'd go crazy if they didn't come in, and it's true. Many people view their workouts as therapeutic, but few workouts can relieve tension better than releasing all of your aggression on an uncomplaining, vinyl-covered bag.

I know it's worked for me. Now, I'm the guy flying through the air and kicking people in the head, and it turns out that 9-year-old was right—it is pretty cool. It's a lot of work, but it's a blast. And I hope as we move through the fundamentals of kickboxing together, you find yourself not just learning a new sport, physical workout or self-defense technique, but discovering a new source of fulfillment as well.

SECTION I

THE FOUNDATION

BACKGROUND

I've used the term "traditional martial arts" when discussing such disciplines as Karate or Tae Kwon Do, which might have given you the impression kickboxing isn't a recognized martial art, that maybe it's just something my friends and I cooked up because we're good at it. That's certainly not the case.

The original form of kickboxing got its start in Thailand and is called Muay Thai, or Thai Boxing. It's the national sport of Thailand, where it enjoys a near fanatical following. There's really nothing to compare the passion the Thai feel for Muay Thai to in North American sports, but if you think of how the more intense South American countries feel about soccer, you start to get the impression.

Muay Thai can trace its roots back to ancient Siam. Just how far back no one really knows, but legends suggest it dates back at least to the late 1500s, probably as a form of military training. Stories from this time say King Naresuen the Great, ancient kickboxing hotshot, enjoyed great success competing in Muay Thai contests, becoming a national hero in his early twenties.

The sport became popular as a Siamese pastime during a peaceful period in the 1700s, and prize fights were common. Combatants wrapped their fists in horsehide or rope to protect their hands and inflict maximum damage on their opponents. Before you flinch at the viciousness of these fights, remember how popular bare-knuckle boxing once was in the West. The thrill of the battle seems to run deep in the human heart.

Muay Thai hasn't changed much since then. Well, boxing gloves were introduced around the 1970s, so the horsehide and rope stuff is gone, but the intensity's still high. Because of its near "anything goes" approach to the use of knees, elbows and kicks to the legs, many people consider Muay Thai the most brutal sport in the world.

In the late 1960s and early 1970s, Europeans and North Americans became more involved in Muay Thai, as well as the Japanese version of kickboxing, which usually didn't allow elbow or knee strikes. But the real interest during this time was in tournament karate, fueled in part by the success of martial arts movies, particularly Bruce Lee movies, like my favorite, *Enter the Dragon*. They sure got my attention.

Tournament karate was noticeably different from kickboxing. In traditional karate tournaments the combatants wore *gi*, the Japanese name for the cotton uniform, and the goal of each contestant was to score points by executing a punch or kick to a vital target area of his opponent, but with enough control that little or no contact was actually made. That's not to say there was never any contact. As anyone who competed back then will tell you, there was plenty, some shots more "accidental" than others. The tournaments were usually held in a hardwood-floored gymnasium, with little fanfare. It was in these humble circumstances that people like Chuck Norris first gained notoriety.

Then along came a man named Jhoon Rhee, who invented a form of protective gear that would change karate tournaments worldwide. The gear was made of foam rubber, and it was designed to cover the hands and feet of the user, but still allow him or her enough mobility to form all the necessary positions to punch and kick. The idea was to

protect competitors if they were on the receiving end of a punch or kick that came too close or landed too hard.

Although protective gear was a noble thought, it seemed to have just the opposite effect than intended. In time, the protective gear, which tournament promoters generally required competitors to wear, seemed to give some users the notion they could hit harder because they were wearing protective gear!

This gear helped spawn a new type of martial arts competition, primarily in North America, that was sort of a cross between boxing and tournament karate. This new style, called full-contact karate, had its awkward moments. Some competitors found it strange to make certain traditional kicking and striking techniques work while wearing the protective equipment. Even the equipment itself could be confusing. The now-standard training gear was in its infancy then, and many competitors didn't know what to make of it. Some would wear the new hand and foot protection, while others would go with boxing gloves and tennis shoes. It was interesting, to say the least.

As full-contact became more refined as a sport and grew in popularity, participants had the opportunity to travel the globe and compete in other countries against other stylists, often under a different set of rules. This

often meant a painful introduction the use of kicks to the legs, what are commonly referred to as "leg kicks." Leg kicks are kicks to any part of the leg—the thighs, knees and calves. These brutal but effective kicks are still not accepted practice in all types of kickboxing.

Most Western full-contact rules only allowed kicks to the opponent's waist and up, with the occasional foot-to-foot sweep, and many of these fighters simply had no idea how to deal with being kicked in the thigh or calf, much less being kneed or elbowed. The results were obvious: Many Western fighters limped home, and a distinct difference of opinion was formed where competitive

rules were concerned. This difference exists to this day.

Even as kickboxing continues to grow and evolve, there are two major schools of thought where the rules are concerned, primarily concerning the use of leg kicks. In most matches outside of Thailand, knees and elbows are considered excessive for competition purposes, but the sport is somewhat divided over kicks to the leg. The term "full-contact" is no longer used and, regardless of the rules, kickboxing as an international sport is here to stay.

Western kickboxing, what used to be known as full-contact karate, is a modern style of kickboxing. Fighters kick from the waist up, no elbows, no knees, no leg kicks, no grabbing. It's straight boxing and high kicks—a softer style of kickboxing. Soft styles of martial arts consist of flowing moves and contained techniques, such as those used in Tai Chi. These styles are circular, with flowing open-hand strikes and soft slaps with the hands. A hard style of martial arts uses closed fists, hard punches, and direct straight-line hard kicks.

On the other end of the spectrum, Muay Thai kickboxing is a hard style of martial arts in which just about anything goes. In competition you'll see the standard kicks and punches as well as leg kicks, use of knees and elbows and grabbing or holding.

Kickboxing bouts are structured much like boxing matches, with rounds of two or three minutes with a rest period between each round. Matches take place in standard boxing rings, and each fighter has two or three corner men. The combatants wear regulation boxing gloves, and, depending on the rules of the individual match, may wear shin or foot protectors.

Fighters sometimes wear long pants made of satin or other materials, but many fighters just wear flashy shorts, made popular by the kickboxers of Thailand. The bouts are judged a lot like boxing matches, with points awarded by judges for execution of technique, aggressiveness, offensive and defensive skill and overall poise in the ring. And as with Western boxing, knocking out your opponent is the most direct path to victory. When I say Western boxing, I mean traditional boxing with just the hands.

Boxing and kickboxing matches can look very similar because they use the same type of ring, ropes, bells, bright baggy shorts, footwork and punches. Maybe these similarities have led to the affinity boxers and kickboxers seem to have for each other. I've always admired Sugar Ray Leonard, a well-rounded boxer with slick tricks. He was a very intelligent fighter who even went to college for a little while. I read a lot about him when I was just starting off as a fighter, and I got good marks in school. He was my hero and I wanted to emulate him.

I have always been a great fan of stylish, smart fighters such as Sugar Ray, Muhammad Ali, Benny "the Jet," Bruce Lee and Bill "Superfoot" Wallace, and tried to emulate them. In fact, my nickname is a play off Sugar Ray's because we have similar styles.

One thing you'll learn quickly is that everybody gets a nickname in boxing and martial arts and the nickname is usually a commentary on your style. For instance, you don't expect John "the Stud" Magichi or Ricky "Bulldog" Pastrami to look nice. Johnny "Twinkletoes" Silversteen, he'll be dancing round the ring.

During my fights, I dance around the ring just out of reach, looking for the opportunity to slip in devastating punches and kicks, but I'm smart and technically correct. At first, everyone called me the Disco Kid: "The Disco Kid Dances to Victory." But at the gym they used to call me Sugar Ray, too. "Sugar Ray" Pete Cunningham. Well, that was someone else's name, so they eventually adapted it to "Sugarfoot" and the name stuck.

One of my specialties in the kickboxing ring are what are called trick kicks. Your standard kicks are round kicks, front kicks and back kicks. Trick kicks look like fakes, something you would see in a movie. You might throw three kicks before setting your leg back on the floor. The first two would fake him out, then, bam, hit him with the last one.

Trick kicks are for points, more or less. You put on a good show for the audience, and pretty soon the audience is cheering for you. These are also a Bill Wallace trademark. It's style. You'll also see trick kicks in martial arts demonstrations, they look great, but people say, "Does that really work?" Yes, it does. But, you won't be learning these quite yet. You'll need a good grounding in the fundamentals before moving on to more complicated moves such as those.

That's the background; now let's get on with the nuts and bolts.

CONDITIONING

Let's get started by discussing methods of training and conditioning, including supplemental training and nutrition. These aspects of a training program are often thought to be necessary only for a more serious-minded athlete or competitor, but not for someone looking for general fitness or recreation. I don't really agree with this way of thinking.

You don't have to be a world-class athlete to train like one, nor do you have to compete just because you could. Regardless of your personal goals, you'll benefit more from your training if you adhere to a training regimen that contains the basic components of fitness, such as flexibility, muscular development and cardiovascular endurance. This is the whole idea behind "cross training," and the kickboxer stands to gain as much as any other athlete.

CARDIOVASCULAR ENDURANCE

For cardiovascular conditioning, running is probably the most important exercise you'll need to do in addition to your kickboxing work. To start off, running three days a week is probably enough. A distance of three miles at a moderate pace every other day, such as Monday-Wednesday-Friday or Tuesday-Thursday-Saturday is recommended. You may get tired in the first one, two, or even three months, running and training, but after a while you get over that hump, and you'll be better for it.

Your primary goals are to keep your weight down and your cardiovascular endurance up. A good pair of running shoes is a must, and, if possible, avoid running on pavement or other hard surfaces, as they can be hard on your joints. Instead, look for a park or similar area that has grass or dirt trails to run on. Hills and beaches provide variety to your workout if you have either of these available to you. Try to run in the early morning or the evening, especially if you live in an urban area; the air is cleaner during those times of the day.

For some, running is simply not an option. Low arches in their feet, a tendency toward shin splints or pain in the knee joints are conditions that may prevent some people from being able to run. If this is the case, I recommend swimming as an alternative to running. There is virtually no stress to the body and it's a great way to build your cardiovascular endurance. I know several good kickboxers who use swimming for their cardio workouts, and it works well for them.

FLEXIBILITY

Stretching is an essential part of your training program as well, both in terms of your running and your kicking. You can stretch every day, but you'll want to vary the stretches slightly and stretch harder on some days than others. Everyone is different, so you'll  want to experiment to see what works best for you. You might try stretching the most on the days that you're going to be doing a lot of kicking. Allow some extra time on these days, you'll need to do some extra repetitions. I recommend stretching with a partner; you'll stretch further faster. Be sure to stretch before you run as well, focusing on the quadriceps, hamstrings and calf muscles.

Weight training is an area where opinion varies greatly. Some fighters say it's an absolute must, claiming the benefits of increased power and self confidence, while others stick to a more old-fashioned school of thought that says it makes a fighter tight and stiff, robbing him of his mobility and speed.

I've never lifted weights myself. As a lightweight fighter, I've never felt the need for it, and at this point in my career I can't see myself pushing iron when I could be pumping out punches. I rely on my calisthenics, such as push-ups and pull-ups, to strengthen my body, as well as practicing on the heavy bag and the Thai pads to work the leverage and power of my techniques.

I must ask that this be taken with a grain of salt, though, as I know many fighters in various weight classes that do very well with a weight program. Most of them do high repetitions with lighter weights for muscle stamina and explosive strength, which go hand-in-hand with fighting.

I do a lot of natural calisthenics. Pushing my own body weight doing push-ups, squats, pull-ups, sit-ups, anything to give added strength. What you're really looking for is more muscle stamina than brute strength. Brute strength comes in handy, but if you fight, you're throwing a bunch of punches in the course of that fight, sometimes 50 in a round. You may be throwing a thousand punches in the course of a fight. For that, you need muscle stamina.

And stamina really shows in the ring. In the first round the brute's punches are good and crisp, all 50. But in the tenth round, his hands are lagging on the ground and he can't get one off. Now a guy who did his homework, who did his pull-ups, who did his push-ups no matter how hard or how bad the burning got, he's still crisp. He's got stamina, not just big old strength.

The one guy might be able to knock a house down, but he's got no stamina because he's got, pant, no, pant, cardio. Now he can only throw three punches. His muscles are hurting, they're weak and tired because he's got no stamina in them. Maybe the other guy can't crack an egg, but he can throw a thousand punches. I'll put my money on him. You need the muscular and cardio stamina.

THE TRAINING PROGRAM

If possible, split your training into sessions that accommodate your schedule and your goals. Start with your cardio, your running and some stretching and calisthenics in the morning. Fighters in training should let

five or six hours pass before starting their gym work; those that work during the day can continue their training in the evening. You'll probably find that alternating the components of your workout, along with the intensity of each session, produces the best results and will help keep things interesting.

Let's look at an average kickboxing workout. One day I might have you warm up for 10 to 20 minutes, followed by jumping rope for another 10 to 20 minutes. You move on to shadowboxing for three rounds, working the hands first, then adding kicks, then both.

If you're not sparring that day, I'd put you on the heavy bag for the hardest work of the day. From there you would move to the focus mitts to work the accuracy of your punches and practice the evasive movements of the head and upper body. Or you may opt for the Thai pads, a larger, rectangular shaped pad worn on the forearms of your coach. These pads are small enough to allow you to practice your punching, yet large enough and solid enough to permit practice of the power kicks, such as the front kick, spinning back kick and the switch

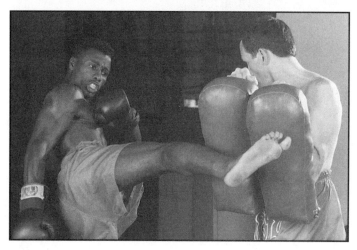

step and whipping round kicks. We'll be discussing all of this equipment at length a little later. After this you could do some light work with a partner, working drills such as combinations or counters.

You would finish up with some exercises such as push-ups and your abdominal work—crunches, leg raises, something like that. Then some stretching to cool down, and you're through. If you plan to spar that day, you would do your stretching, your jumping rope, your shadowboxing, then head to the ring. After three or four rounds of sparring you won't need to work the heavy bag, I'd work you on the mitts or Thai pads, or both. Partner work wouldn't be necessary since you sparred, so you would finish up with your calisthenics and your cool down stretches.

I suggest that you write down your schedule and discuss it with your coach or instructor. Alternate the activities so that you don't do the same type or same intensity of work two days in a row. Enthusiasm is a great asset, but common sense and intelligent training methods are necessary to produce the desired results.

Try to plan your personal schedule to take all of these factors into consideration. If you intend to really go for it, plan on training five days a week, with two off to rest and let the body heal and recuperate. If you're not already on a workout program, I'd advise keeping it to three days a week, to avoid burnout or muscle soreness. Space a day in-between each workout to give your body a rest.

NUTRITION

With all of the energy expended in a rigorous training program, your diet becomes a very important part of the overall picture. A poor diet can sabotage all of your hard work. You're training your body to be a Porsche, and then you pour in some diesel fuel! It won't go. Bang, bang, bang. All kinds of trouble. You want premium fuel all the way.

There is a wealth of information available on nutrition, and I suggest you make use of it. Again, some experimentation will probably be necessary for you to determine what is best for you in terms of calorie consumption and protein-to-carbohydrate ratios.

I generally try to keep my intake of fats down, along with caffeine and sugar. Poultry and fish are good sources of protein that are low in fat. A very lean steak is a good source of iron, a necessary nutrient. Fruits and vegetables are an essential part of the diet, and I also enjoy brown rice and pasta dishes. Fruit juices are good, although I recommend drinking them diluted with water to about half strength. I supplement my diet with a multi-vitamin, as well as with amino acids and electrolytes. And don't forget to drink plenty (I mean lots) of water.

GETTING 3 STARTED

Now it's time to get serious. This kickboxing stuff is for real, and it's going to take some commitment. You have to ask yourself, "Am I willing to put some time into this thing?"

Even if your goal is just to be able to look after yourself, you're going to have to put in some time. You may have to drop something, maybe give up a sport or going out for that drink on Friday night. There are a lot of things that don't go together with being in shape, and many of them are fun.

Also, you are going to get bumps and bruises, and maybe a few sore muscles, along the line. Are you willing to take some?

But the most important reason to decide to train in kickboxing isn't to compete, or to be in shape or to put a mugger in the hospital. It's to have fun. If you think you'll enjoy this, let's go. If you're forcing yourself to train as a kickboxer, I'd rather you found a different way to torture yourself, because you'll only bring the rest of us down.

Now that you've decided to train in kickboxing, you have some important choices to make. You'll need to find a place to train, a school or gym that suits your needs. You'll need to invest in some equipment, and, perhaps most important, you'll need good instruction and some partners to train with.

I was fortunate in the early days of my training to have instructors who were not only very adept in the art of Chito-Ryu, a hard style of karate, but were liberal enough in their thinking to see the advantages of boxing as well. I give Robert Supeen, Sr., and Robert Supeen, Jr., a lot of credit for giving me a push in that direction. I competed in my first traditional karate tournament at the age of 14. The following year, at the age of 15, I made the transition to kickboxing training. My instructors felt I had the heart and the talent to go forward, so they pushed me very fast, and I was glad for the opportunity.

CHOOSING A SCHOOL AND TEACHER

Things have changed considerably from when I started training. Today, there are gyms where you can get good kickboxing training that includes a solid traditional base, a quality boxing coach, and extensive fitness programs, such as weight training and aerobics. This is quite a change from my early days of training, when the boxing gym was down the street from the karate school, and the fitness place was two blocks further and around the corner. It was a workout just making the rounds. Gyms today have broadened their appeal, and you can probably find everything you need under one roof.

If you can't find a suitable all-in-one gym, look for a good boxing gym and do some training that involves your hands only. I really can't stress enough the importance of developing your boxing skills along with your kicking skills. The hands are often overlooked when kicking is involved, but they are every bit as important.

At this point, if you are a novice kickboxer, you should start defining your personal goals. Put some thought into why you want to train and what you hope to achieve from it. Do you have any competitive aspirations, or are you merely trying to get in shape? Are you looking to round out your martial arts repertoire, or are you focusing on self-defense? These are all valid goals, and while they'll only make a little difference in how you proceed, it's important for you to know what you're after.

You also need to start exploring different schools. Shop around, check the yellow pages and see what's available and how much lessons will cost. Martial arts supply stores can be excellent sources of information about existing schools and gyms.

Drop in unannounced at potential schools so you get an idea of how the school is really run. Ask yourself some questions: What are the instructors like? How many are there? What are their qualifications?

A skilled teacher is very important. He may have been a world champion, maybe not. It really doesn't matter. The greatest coaches are not necessarily the greatest fighters. You may find a guy who didn't even compete as an amateur, but teaches good strong techniques and gets the message across to his students.

Sometimes the former champion doesn't make the best teacher, because a large part of his success was talent rather than technique. No one can teach you talent, so look for someone strong on technique.

While you're visiting, check out the students as well. Remember, these are the people you'll be training with. Do they look like people you can work with? Are there any "loose cannons" in the class you would want to avoid? Talk to the students after class and get their feedback.

The students are what make a good school. Are they where you want to be?

Is the overall atmosphere a comfortable one? It can be a beautiful building, have nice sparring facilities, but if the sensei's rough or abrasive, will they matter? You will find egomaniacs in martial arts. There is a difference between ego and respect, and if you're not comfortable with the sensei's approach to the two, you won't be happy with the school. You need a good relationship between the instructor and the student.

Where is the school located, and what is the class schedule like? Is the neighborhood a place you would be comfortable traveling to and from? These are the types of questions you should ask yourself, and you should add a number of your own.

It used to be, schools would run each other down. While I can't say that no longer happens, I can tell you what a good school should say: "Go and check around, then come back. If you think we're the people for you, then we're the people for you. If not, we will understand." That's a good gym. And beware of the high-pressure, good-only-for-the-next-hour deals some gyms throw at you. If it's a good gym, the deal should be the same tomorrow or next week as it is right this minute.

BUYING EQUIPMENT

Finally, you'll need to invest in some equipment. I say invest because that's exactly what it is—an investment. Some schools will have a hundred gloves on the wall, all the different sizes, maybe a hundred pads, too. Remember now, you use the gloves and pads, and so does Frank, and so does Jane, and so does Suzy. Everyone using the same equipment gets it, shall we say, a little damp. It's best to have your own stuff and keep it clean.

Good equipment is essential to preventing injury. Usually, the gym has a pro shop, but the prices are not the best you can get. Look for kickboxing equipment in specialty shops and catalogs. You need the equipment before you start. Basic personal equipment you'll need to purchase are hand wraps, boxing gloves, mouthpiece, head protection, groin (or chest) protection, foot protection, shin protection and shorts.

Usually, when I walk into the gym the first thing I do is put my hand wraps on and warm up. Then, if I'm going into the ring, I grab my headgear, my mouthpiece and my Vaseline, which keeps me from getting scarred up by encouraging any errant gloves to slide off my face. I fill my water bottle, and leave it sitting by the ring so I can take a little sip between rounds. I put on my gear, my groin protection, my shin gear and my boxing gloves, and I'm ready to go.

A good pair of boxing gloves will be one of your biggest expenditures, but they're a classic example of "you get what you pay for." A well-built pair will literally last you years, while a cheap pair may last through only a few months of hard training.

Purchase your gloves from a boxing gym or catalog, as the ones sold in sporting goods stores usually aren't made very well. Your gloves should weigh between 14 and 16 ounces each, and be made of leather with plenty of padding across the knuckles.

Give any boxing gloves the "squeeze" test before you purchase them. Put one glove on and grab it with your bare hand, with your fingers on the palm side and your thumb over the part of the glove that covers your knuckles. Squeeze with your thumb; there should be enough padding that your thumb sinks in only slightly. If you can feel your knuckles through the glove, look for better equipment.

Buy a pair of gloves with the thumb protector. Without it your thumb may stick out just a little. If you throw a punch and miss by just so much, your thumb will hook up on the side of your opponent's head and you'll crack your thumb all the way back. Ouch!

Many boxing gloves today have Velcro closures instead of laces. These are very convenient and work well, but you want to make sure they are closed correctly so your partner won't be scraped or scratched by the Velcro.

If you or your partner use lace-up gloves, tuck the excess string into the crisscrossed part of the laces or tape over them to prevent them from coming undone and possibly whipping someone in the eye. Your boxing gloves are one of your most essential pieces of equipment—shop around and invest in a well-made pair that will last.

You should get a pair of bag gloves or a second pair of boxing gloves for working on the focus mitts and heavy bag. Don't use your sparring gloves for this supplemental work; the bags will quickly rough up your gloves.

You'll also need a pair of wraps for your hands. Hand wraps protect your hands, adding an additional layer of padding inside your boxing gloves. They are long, thin strips of cloth or gauze with a loop on one end.

There are two basic types of hand wraps, the standard wrap and the kind that's sometimes called the Mexican handwrap. The standard type is usually made of a thicker material than the Mexican style, which is longer in length than the standard. Which you use is a matter of preference; you may want to purchase a pair of each and see which one you like best.

I prefer the Mexican wraps. Boxing is almost a national sport in Mexico, much like Thailand with its kickboxing, and the Mexicans have spent extra time and effort developing proper wraps and gauze for the hands. The Mexican wrap is a flexible gauze-type fabric that pads your hands better and cushions them better.

To wrap your hands, start with your left hand first. Place your thumb in the loop of one wrap and pull the strip down across the back of your wrist. Circle your wrist with the wrap, keeping it snug, straight and wrinkle-free. Circle your forearm with the

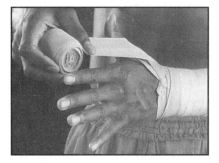

wrap about one-third of the way down your forearm then back up to your wrist.

Circle your thumb once then go back to where you left off at your wrist and circle your wrist.
Do this twice more,

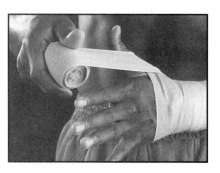

then circle around your first set of knuckles, across the top of your knuckles and around the outside of your pinky. Pull the wrap

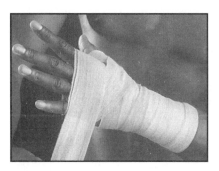

from your pinky across the palm of your hand to the base of your thumb and back over the top of your hand

through the gap between your pinky and your ring finger. Continue around and through the gaps between each successive finger.
Circle your hand across

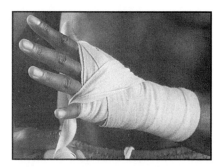

your knuckles once more, then pull the wrap down to your forearm, circle it and secure the wrap.

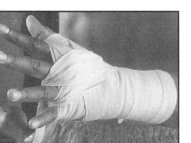

This is a typical wrap sequence. Usually, you'll learn how to wrap your hands from your teacher and adjust the wrapping style to whatever is most comfortable for you.

A good headgear is probably the single most important piece of equipment you will own, although some fighters I know would argue that this distinction belongs to the protective cup. In recent years there's been tremendous growth in the types and varieties of protective equipment available, and this includes headgear.

I prefer the standard boxing type myself, but some headgear have a piece that protects the chin and jaw, much like a motorcycle helmet, while others completely encase the head like a Medieval helmet. Most are adjustable so you can customize the fit. Always try to purchase yours from a store that allows you to try it on first. Wearing headgear is not a natural feeling, and you should be comfortable with your selection. Also, some headgear restrict your vision more than others, and that's the last thing you want when someone's trying to kick you in the head!

Along with a headgear, you'll need a good mouthpiece. Since the top of the line mouthpieces are only a few dollars, buy the best one possible. Considering what they protect, it's money well spent. You may wish to consider a mouthpiece that's custom-molded to fit your teeth. These are very popular and readily available.

Always use your mouthpiece; even if you're just doing jumping jacks, you can chip a tooth. Also, you should get used to the mouthpiece in practice and training before you get into the ring with it—it can be awkward at first. You're supposed to breathe through your nose and keep your mouth closed, but you've got this big old thing in your mouth and your face is all puffed up. When you start sparring, it can be claustrophobic, "I can't breathe." Breathe through your nose, and you'll quickly forget you're wearing it.

A protective cup or groin protection is a must for any male participating in any type of contact sport, particularly kickboxing. Again, cups are relatively inexpensive and available at most sporting goods stores. I prefer the boxing type of groin protector that's worn over the clothing. These offer maximum protection, and some are designed with the kicker in mind, with the hip protection removed to allow the legs room to kick. Women can purchase specially designed chest protectors.

Shin pads are good for sparring and partner drills, although I don't recommend you wear them while practicing your kicks on any type of bag or pad. You should try to toughen up your shins gradually, and wearing shin pads too often defeats this purpose. A large variety of shin pads are on the market, so you should have no trouble finding a pair you like.

Foot protection, although available, is not necessary. Also, whether you wear shoes while you train is largely a matter of personal preference. I do the bulk of my training in the gym barefoot, as I'm barefoot when I compete in the ring and I like to keep my training as realistic as possible. Kicking with shoes on may throw your timing off, and sometimes they don't allow you to form the proper weapons with your feet. But again, it's a matter of preference.

Training gear is designed to protect the person you're working or sparring with as much as it's designed to protect you, but this is often overlooked. Many people don't realize that, while their gear might feel sufficiently padded to them, it may not feel that way to the person they're hitting.

TRAINING WITH A PARTNER

When your training progresses to the point where you're doing drill work with another person or actually sparring, choose the people you work with wisely. Try to work with people that are of a similar skill level as you, yet still cause you to work hard to keep up with them.

In a classroom situation, you won't always be able to control who you work with, so you'll need to be able to derive some benefit from working with just about anyone. But whenever possible, work with people that bring out the best in you. This doesn't mean working with people with a skill level lower than yours just to make yourself look good. Working at your lowest level only limits your growth and hurts you in the long run.

Before doing any sort of contact drills, and especially before sparring, check your partner's equipment. In particular, give his boxing gloves the squeeze test. If you can feel his knuckles through his glove, you may not want to work with him until he gets better equipment. Remember, it won't be your fingers you'll be feeling those knuckles on.

And be on the lookout for that "loose cannon" I mentioned earlier. You'll know him when you see him—he's the guy with the real "banzai" approach to his training. He usually lacks self-control and often he's more dangerous when you're working drills or holding the pads for him than when you're sparring with him. Keep your eye on this one. To a certain degree,  injuries are inevitable when you train in a contact sport, but you don't have to go looking for them. This fellow is liable to hurt you without even realizing it. But I always say, if he cracks you hard, crack him back! He'll probably get the point. If he doesn't, take it up with the instructor in private.

There must always be a sense of give and take when working with other students, but there's no reason for you to take more than you give. If you come across individuals you feel are unsafe to work with, don't. And don't get so enthusiastic in your training that *you* become the loose cannon.

CRITICAL POINTS

The body is critical to a kickboxer. You must know the human body well enough to keep yours in shape and to shoot for the most vulnerable targets on your opponent's. You must also respect your opponent enough not to permanently injure him, unless of course, it's a street thug with a pipe. You must also understand which parts of your body make the best weapons and which targets are available for each punch and kick.

CRITICAL BODY POINTS

To condition and train your body for kickboxing you must concentrate on three areas: legs and butt, stomach and back, and arms and shoulders. Let's start from the ground up and review the major muscle groups. Legs are always important. A good trainer once pointed out to me that anyone working out, doing the drills, doing the kicks everyday builds his legs naturally.

The major muscle groups in the legs are the calf muscles, which pull you up on your toes; the shin muscles (yes, you have muscles there), which pull the toes up toward the knee; the quadriceps along the top of your thigh straighten the knee and help pull your legs up toward your chest; the hamstrings, on the back of the thigh and knee, bend your knee; the inner thigh or adductors, bring your legs together; and the ever-popular *gluteus maximus,* or butt muscles, pull your legs backward.

An area that's ignored and usually a little soft is the stomach. While conditioning, you have to concentrate on developing the armor here because you'll be taking the kicks, never mind punches, to the belly. You need a strong midsection to ward off the attacks, a little armor. Muscle

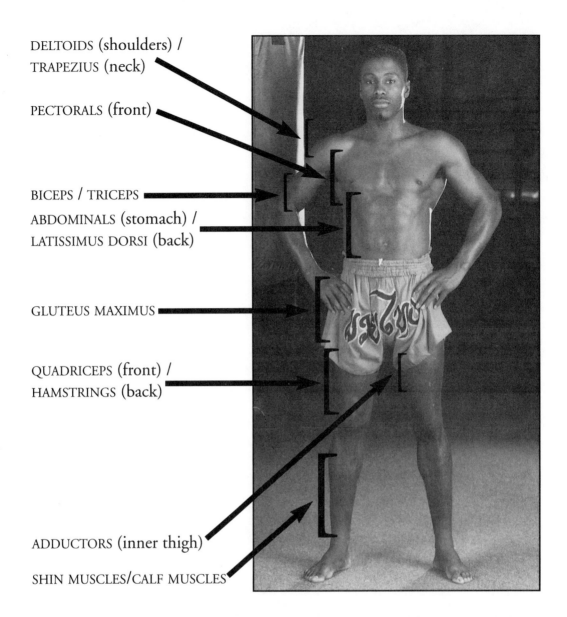

DELTOIDS (shoulders) /
TRAPEZIUS (neck)

PECTORALS (front)

BICEPS / TRICEPS

ABDOMINALS (stomach) /
LATISSIMUS DORSI (back)

GLUTEUS MAXIMUS

QUADRICEPS (front) /
HAMSTRINGS (back)

ADDUCTORS (inner thigh)

SHIN MUSCLES/CALF MUSCLES

groups in the stomach are called abdominals or *rectus abdominus,* and along your chest are the pectorals, which pull arms up, forward and in. Along your back, the large central muscle, which pulls the arms down, is the *latissimus dorsi;* along the shoulders and down the center of the back is the *trapezius,* which pulls your shoulders down and back; and on top of your shoulders are the deltoids, which lift the arms out and to the sides.

Along your arms, the main muscle in the back of your arms is the tricep, which straightens your elbows. Along the front of your arms the main muscle is the bicep, which bends your elbows, and along your wrist are smaller muscles too numerous to mention.

You must isolate your pectorals, triceps, deltoids and lats. That's where your power comes from for punching. When you plan your conditioning schedule, concentrate on these areas because you're going to need these for punching power. Even though kickboxing is a finesse sport, you need something to fire with; the muscle groups in the arms, shoulders neck and head—front and back.

BASIC PUNCHES AND KICKS

Now to give you an idea of the parts of the body you'll be using as weapons and targets, let's review the basic kicks and punches. Don't forget about your elbows and knees. They're powerful weapons that can't be ignored. These quick descriptions are just an overview of your fundamental techniques. We'll go into them in more detail later.

The *front kick* is a set-up kick thrown straight out from your body, usually using the ball of your foot as the striking surface in a snapping or thrusting motion. You snap either leg out to your opponent's solar plexus or chin, the two primary targets for this kick, but you can aim this kick just about anywhere.

The *side kick* is fast and powerful and can be thrown sideways from the body with either leg in a snapping or thrusting motion to the waist, solar plexus, chest and the face. Your kicking foot is parallel to the floor, and the striking area, the side of your foot and the heel, points toward your opponent.

The *hook kick,* sometimes called a reverse roundhouse, comes from above the opponent's head and can knock him out. It is thrown with either leg using the point of your heel to strike the target, usually your opponent's jaw or temple.

The *spinning back kick* is a power kick thrust back from your body. The foot is usually toes down with the heel pointing up, using the bottom of the heel to strike his ribs, solar plexus or lower abdomen. It can also be thrown with the kicking foot parallel to the floor at the midsection, chest or head.

The *round kick,* or roundhouse, is a basic kick thrown with either leg, using your shin or instep to strike your opponent's head, legs or midsection.

The *jab* is a set-up punch thrown straight out from face level. It can be thrown with either hand to your opponent's face, usually the jaw, nose or either eye, or his body.

The *right cross,* or straight right, is a power punch used for knockouts. Equally effective to the head and body, it is thrown with the right arm, which follows a straight path from your shoulder to your opponent's head.

The *hook* is a knockout punch effective to the body or head and thrown with either hand. The left arm comes up parallel to the ground and goes to the chin or jaw or to your opponent's midsection, to either side of his body or to his kidney areas.

The *uppercut* is nasty when used to an opponent's chin, and is a set-up for a finishing hook. It can be thrown to the body, usually the solar plexus, or to the chin with either hand with equal results. The uppercut comes from your waist area up, with the palm of your hand facing you.

The *overhand right* is a variation of the right cross that follows a curved path to the temple, side of the jaw or the ear. It is thrown from just above and to the right of your head in a curved path toward your opponent's head and lands with the knuckles of your fist down.

The *straight, or inside knee, and the side, or outside knee* can be thrown with either knee. The straight knee is thrown with a bent leg, driving your hips forward, striking with the point of your knee to your opponent's midsection or the front of your opponent's thigh. The outside knee goes out to the side of the body and is then pulled in to the opponent's floating ribs, using the inside of the knee joint as the striking surface.

Elbows are thrown using the bony point of either elbow as the striking surface. The horizontal elbow is thrown from the front or rear to the point of your opponent's jaw. With the vertical elbow, the point of your elbow comes up under the point of your opponent's chin, and the diagonal elbow follows a line from above the eye down across the bridge of the nose.

Striking Surfaces and Primary Targets

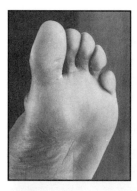

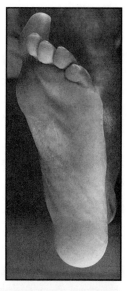

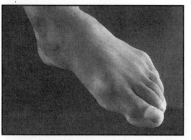

With all these basic striking techniques, you must use certain parts of your body to deliver the most force without injuring yourself. Starting again with your legs, striking surfaces you want to use are the balls of your feet, the bottoms of your feet, your heels (bottom and back or hammer-style), insteps, shins and knees (front, top and sides). These are your lower weapons.

Hands, next. When punching, form a fist and use the first two punch knuckles (the largest two knuckles). Try to hit square with these every time, not the small ones, especially when hitting the head. If you hit with the small knuckles, you'll break them.

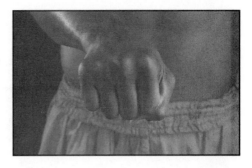

Moving up the arms, the elbows are particularly dangerous weapons. I'll teach you to use these for use on the street and in self-defense, but in the ring, you'll rarely see them allowed. Use the bony point, and the top and bottom of your elbow to strike.

Now, take a look at the most vulnerable points on your opponent's body. These are the areas you will consistently aim for to do the most damage. Looking at lower body targets, you'll use mostly your kicks and knees, and occasionally an elbow. Targets, from the floor up, are the calves, inside and outside, and the knee.

Be careful when kicking to the knee, a good strike here can cause permanent damage. In a fight, you don't have to go for the knee, well, if it's poking out, okay, kick his knee. On the street, do what you have to do. From there, strike the thighs, inside and outside, but stay away from the groin in the ring, it's illegal. You can also use a good straight knee to strike the front of his thigh.

To your opponent's midsection, kick, punch, knee and elbow his solar plexus, chest, kidneys and ribs. If you're coming straight on you'd use kicks that go straight through, like a stomp, or sideways through his defenses striking with the ball of your foot or your heel. These kicks include the front kick, side kick and spinning back kick. Other techniques to throw straight into the midsection or head are the jab, uppercut and right cross. Use your knee to his solar plexus and chest.

To the sides, use the round kick, hook kick, knees and elbows. When kicking to the legs, to the calves or to the thighs, the striking surface is your lower shin. Also use your instep, to the inside it has a stinging effect. When kicking to the body, round house kicks come to the outside, and you can use your foot, your instep, or your shin as the striking surface. When going with a round kick to the head, same thing, using a winging motion. With high spinning or hook kicks you can go to the temples, the ears and the back or side of the neck with your heel.

Knees go to the outside of the body, usually the floating ribs, sometimes his pecs, and the elbows go the to point of the chin, the temples, eyes, nose and ears. Knee him in the head by tipping him to the side, using the side of your knee, or square in the face if you can get a jumping knee.

You can hurt your opponent by shooting for all the targets mentioned above. However, unless you can get that knockout power punch through, you'll have to go for a battering ram effect, bruising and hammering your opponent until he makes a dangerous mistake or drops out of the fight.

WARMING UP

Warming up is kind of like your insurance policy against injury. It's important to take a few minutes to properly warm up the muscles of your body just before you start your workout, especially in the early stages of a training program. It's not very exciting, but the one time you go without you'll probably regret it. A good warm up is one of the best ways to reduce your chances of being injured.

We're now going to work through a basic program for warming up before training. This is a good, solid approach that covers the body from head to toe.

Without downplaying the importance of a good warm up, I must say that time spent warming up is often not used to its fullest potential. It's easy to get down on the floor and do some nice, relaxed stretching, taking your time and easing yourself into your workout. The only problem with this is that you may find you've been down on the floor a lot longer than you had intended, and your workout time is slipping away.

Regardless of whether I'm teaching a class or doing my own training, I like to keep the warm up time to about 15 to 20 minutes. This maximizes the efficiency of the warm up, and helps me to focus on why I'm doing it in the first place.

But don't go to the other extreme, either, and rush through your warm up to get to your workout. You're going to be making some serious demands of your muscles as part of your training—make the time you spend stretching count. You have to be fast to kick somebody in the head, so the muscles are being pulled at rates they're probably not used to travelling at. All of a sudden your leg is accelerating and, pop, you're going to pull something. I've cut 90 percent of my gym-related injuries by stretching.

And let me burst one bubble before we start: If you have the flexibility of spring steel, these exercises will not turn you into a pretzel. Sorry. It may give you the flexibility of warm spring steel, but it's not going to work miracles. Your warm up will reduce the likelihood of injury and probably make you feel better, so don't get greedy.

Lastly, though we've all heard it: Stretch, don't bounce. And don't forget to breathe.

Start at either end of your body and work your way up or down. This keeps you from forgetting any areas. We'll start from the top, and work on loosening and limbering up the neck area first.

Begin by simply moving your head down and back, your chin toward your chest and then toward the ceiling, for three to five repetitions each direction.

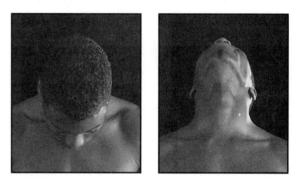

Then move your head to the left, then to the right, three to five times on each side.

Next, try to touch your shoulder with your ear, three to five times on each side. Keep your shoulder down and concentrate on only moving your head.

Finally, rotate your head gently in a circle, three times each direction.

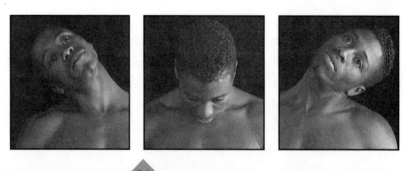

Moving down, the shoulders are next. Try to isolate the movement so that only your shoulders move. This is a light stretch, nothing exaggerated.

Rotate your shoulders in easy circles, back five to 10 times, then forward five to 10 times.

With your arms extended, swing them backwards in a circle at a medium pace for 10 to 15 repetitions, then repeat the movement to the front.

With your arms bent and your fists facing each other, extend your elbows back and forward twice, then extend your open arms back on the third count. Do five to 10 reps. You should feel a pull all the way across your chest and arms. This is an extensive stretch.

Now we'll start loosening up the torso and the sides.

Widen your stance to a little wider than shoulder width and extend your arms straight up, grabbing one wrist. Stretch to one side, then grab the other wrist and stretch to the other side, for five reps each.

From the previous stance, bend at the waist and bring your arms in. Keeping your back as straight as possible, rotate your torso five times in each direction.

The hips and pelvic girdle are next.

With your hands on your hips, swing them in a circular motion, five times in each direction. Try to imagine four points—to the front, left side, rear and right side—that you're trying to hit with your hips as you circle them.

Continuing down the body, we'll now start to warm up the lower half.

With your back straight and legs together and bent, place your palms on your legs just above your knees, being careful not to push on your kneecaps. Rotate your knees in a circle to the left and the right, five times each.

Holding one ankle, rotate your foot with your other hand in a circular motion, five times in each direction. Finish the movement by gently pulling the instep of the foot downward. Repeat with the other leg. This exercise allows you to practice your balance while warming up your ankle joints.

Now widen your stance to double shoulder width. Stretch down to one side, grabbing your leg or ankle to pull yourself down. Keep your back as straight as possible. Come up, and repeat the motion on the other side. Hold each side for 15 seconds, exhaling as you go down. Do two reps on each side, alternating side to side. Then repeat the movement to the front, again holding for 15 seconds for two reps.

From a squatting position, extend one leg out to the side with your heel on the floor, toes pointing up. Keep your knee as straight as possible. This stretches the hamstring muscles in the back of your leg. Putting your hands on the floor for balance, if necessary, shift your weight to the other side and extend the other leg. Again, alternate legs and do two reps for 15 seconds each.

Next, do the same movement, only this time position your foot with the toes pointing to the front; this simulates a side kick. Alternate this one as well, with two reps on each side for 15 seconds each.

Next assume a sitting position with the legs out in a wide "V" as far as they will go. With your fingers laced behind your head, bend from side to side, attempting to touch your elbows to your thighs or the floor. Do 10 repetitions each side.

From the same sitting position, reach to the side, face toward your knee, and hold the stretch for 15 seconds. Remember to breathe out as you go down, and keep your knee straight. Alternate your right and left legs twice, then go down to the front for two sets of 15 seconds. Come up, placing your hands flat on the floor behind your back.

Now, push yourself up to a front split position (body facing front), supporting your weight with your hands, then gradually lean your torso forward down to the floor, pushing your pelvis to the floor.
Hold this position for 15 seconds, then push back up to the front splits position.

From here, raise up slightly on your hands and carefully twist your body and legs to the right, into a side splits position. Hold for 15 seconds, then raise up and turn to the other side. Turn back to the front position, and, again supporting yourself with your hands, ease yourself back to a sitting position. Gently push yourself back with your hands, bringing your legs together. This is a safe way to come out of the position that helps prevent muscle pulls.

Sit with your knees bent and your feet flat on the floor. Lie back, then move your knees from side to side for three to five reps each side.

From the sitting position, come up to the balls of your feet, then kneel with the tops of your feet flat on the floor. Supporting yourself with your hands, slowly lean back as far as you can with your knees remaining on the floor. This stretches the quadriceps in the front of your legs. Repeat three times.

To finish the warm up, roll into a ball with your legs tucked to your chin and gently rock on your back to stretch your spine.

You have to push yourself during your stretches. You can't say, "No I'm not going to go past this." You have to say, "Yeah, I'll try." Some of the kicks we'll be doing can't be done unless you're very, very loose. You have to be realistic.

Don't let any difficulty you may have with any of the stretches bother you. Each person will be able to stretch to a different degree, and what matters most is that you give your best effort to stretching your muscles.

If you can't do the splits, don't sweat it. I'm not so hot at the splits myself, and they're definitely not my favorite. It's hard for me to do the straight splits, the Japanese splits, without being assisted. If someone comes behind me and pushes my hips down, I can do them.

When I first started training, all of the other guys were really flexible, and they just took it for granted that I was, too. One day, all of a sudden, while I'm working my way down into the splits, somebody pushed me all the way down to the floor. Oww! Since then, I haven't been too fond of the splits.

But it's not a big deal to not be able to do the splits. It hasn't hurt my career much. A lot of kids starting off believe that you have to do the splits to be a great fighter. "If you can't do the splits like Baryshnikov, forget it," they think. But it's not true. Some of the better fighters in kickboxing can't do the splits to save their lives. But they'll kick you in the leg and knock you silly. So don't get worked up if you're not Mr. or Ms. Flexibility.

You still have to go through the stretching routine though, as it's essential to getting some kicks off and learning the proper technique. And always have a partner help you for more intense stretching, but make sure you're both communicating well as to how far your partner should be pushing.

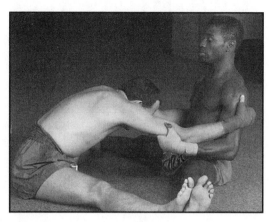

You need to stretch it out, relax that body. Now you've stretched your muscles out, really stretched out and relaxed. Time for calisthenics.

First, I start out with as many push-ups as I can do, keeping my back straight. Then I turn over on my back and do reverse push-ups, again, keeping the body straight. I usually do my abdominals at the end of my workout with a few more calisthenics, but you can do them at the beginning as well. Standard sit-ups, lots of them, do the job. Concentrate on working just the stomach muscle as you come up and back down; don't pull with your neck, back or hands.

Next, I do my squats to work my legs and kicking muscles. This exercise really gets your blood moving, too. Stand with your feet shoulder width apart, bending your arms up. Squat down, then quickly stand back up with one knee bent. When you are fully upright, kick straight out with your bent leg. Bring the leg back to the bent position and squat again. Repeat the motion, using the opposite leg. Do as many as you can.

For last part of my warm up, I jump rope for about five to 10 minutes.

The calisthenics and the warm up pump blood through those muscles. Now you can get to work.

TRAINING WITH 6 EQUIPMENT

What doesn't fight back—usually

Regardless of your personal goals, degree of participation or skill level, your kickboxing training will include working with a variety of equipment, such as heavy bags, focus mitts and kicking pads. This is important because it allows you to practice your punches, kicks, knee and elbow strikes, combinations, blocking, bobbing and weaving without the pressure of having another person punching and kicking back at you.

It also allows your coach or instructor to give you one-on-one feedback about your strengths and weaknesses, and it's a more relaxed atmosphere in general. "Relaxed" doesn't mean easy, however, and you may find that some of your toughest workouts involve working with these types of equipment. The most common types of equipment include the heavy bag, focus mitts, Thai pads and sometimes a kicking shield.

HEAVY BAGS

Heavy bags come in all sizes and shapes, but generally kickboxing schools have two types; the standard 70-pound boxing heavy bag and an elongated version that hangs nearly to the floor and may weigh 100 pounds or more. This longer heavy bag (sometimes called a "banana bag") is designed specifically for kickboxing, and the extra length lets you practice the lower leg kicks. Either heavy bag serves the same purpose: to allow you to develop your power and leverage with punches and kicks.

Heavy bags are usually suspended from the ceiling or a support beam by a strong chain and swivel, in an area that allows the bag some room to swing freely. The standard boxing type was traditionally made of canvas, but today most heavy bags are made of a durable vinyl. Vinyl is more compatible with the materials that bag gloves and shin pads are made of, as the abrasiveness of canvas bags is notorious for ruining fighters' equipment.

Vinyl bags also seem to be more durable and longer lasting, a real benefit when you consider their cost. A heavy bag, used properly, can provide a great conditioning workout by itself, and many fitness clubs are adding heavy bag classes as part of their offered services because of the overall strength-building and cardiovascular benefits.

FOCUS MITTS

As a kickboxer who pays a lot of attention to his boxing skills, I believe focus mitts are invaluable for training your hands. Generally made of leather, they somewhat resemble catcher's mitts and are worn in pairs by a coach or instructor, who uses them

to simulate an opponent's head. They're relatively small, about the size of a man's outstretched hand, and require you to be accurate with your punches.

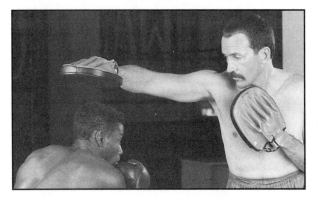

Focus mitts let your coach or trainer move around, making you throw punches from a variety of angles and situations, and they're excellent for practicing your boxing combinations. They're also used to sharpen your defensive skills. Part of a mitt workout should include your coach lightly slapping at you with the mitts, causing you to bob, weave and block. This is a great way to check the guard position of your hands and your reaction time, and it usually exposes any weaknesses in your defense.

A good coach occasionally places the mitts at his sides, so you can practice pinpointing your body shots. Focus mitts are also very useful for practicing high snapping kicks, such as the round kick and the hook kick. Again, their small size makes accuracy a must, and the mitts are

light enough to be easily held high for extended periods of time. Focus mitts, like any piece of equipment that your coach or instructor can use to simulate an opponent's body, position or any attacks he may throw at you, are extremely helpful.

THAI PADS

Thai pads, sometimes called kicking pads, were developed by Muay Thai trainers to give them mobility while drilling their fighters' kicks. Thai pads are roughly rectangular in shape, about 18 to 20 inches long and eight to 10 inches wide. They are very well padded, and almost as thick as they are wide.

The thick padding is for the safety of the person holding the pads, not the person kicking them. With straps and handles securely sewn on to the back, they, too, are worn in pairs by your coach.

In Thailand and other Thai-style schools, the coach also wears a belt with a large round padded front. This padded belt enables the fighter to practice his front kicks realistically without injuring his coach.

A quick training tip: Try to avoid injuring your coach at all costs, as it usually means extra work for you. Coaches have no sense of humor.

While other kicks can be practiced on them, these pads are best suited for the powerful Muay Thai-type round kicks they were designed for. Since they are relatively lightweight and easy to move around with, yet able to withstand very hard kicks, working with a set of Thai pads allows a fighter to combine mobility work and power training into one lesson.

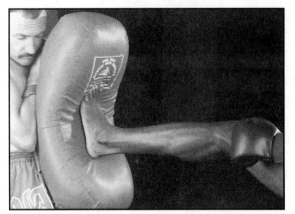

A kicking shield is a large hand-held pad that is used to practice, you guessed it, kicking techniques at full power. It is similar to the pads used by football players to practice blocking skills.

The kicking shield is commonly used in traditional karate schools, but seems to be under-used in kickboxing training. I think this shows a limited perception of kicking. There should be more to kickboxing than a front kick and a power round kick, and if a bigger variety of kicks were used, there would be a greater need for kicking shields. As it stands, this piece of equipment collects too much dust.

The kicking shield is rectangular or oval, between two and two-and-a-half feet long and it curves in at the middle, the spot where your kick should land. This curve helps dissipate the force of the kick for the person holding the shield and keeps your foot and shin from slipping off. If a shield doesn't have this curve, don't use it.

The back of the shield has two side-by-side vertical straps and one horizontal strap or handle to hold it with. The shield is usually a little over a foot wide, about eight inches thick and a good one will weigh between 10 and 15 pounds.

I say "good one" because there's a large quality range in kicking shields. Some are padded with filler material, while others are air-filled. The air-filled ones are too light and flimsy, and I don't think they give the person kicking the shield the right feel. Given the power of the types of kicks usually practiced on it, a kicking shield should provide a firm surface for the person kicking it and good padding for the person holding it.

The shield is ideal for practicing front kicks, side kicks, spinning back kicks, round kicks and shin kicks. Like the other hand-held pads and mitts, it offers the user mobility, making the training more realistic. Also, the kicking shield offers probably the most reliable gauge of your kicking power, usually based upon how far the person holding the shield moved when you kicked it.

MIRROR

One of the most important pieces of equipment you will ever use, strangely enough, is a mirror. This is something boxers have used for years, and it can prove invaluable for the kickboxer as well. The mirror is used for shadowboxing, or in this case, shadowkickboxing. Shadowboxing lets you examine yourself the way your opponents and training partners see you, and it enables you to visualize imaginary opponents and create strategies and combinations to go after them with.

The mirror reveals everything, top to bottom, that you're doing, correct and incorrect. Most serious fighters spend a good amount of their training time in front of a mirror, punching, kicking and moving, all the while looking for flaws to correct or points to improve on. It's especially helpful to check things such as your stance and the position of your guard.

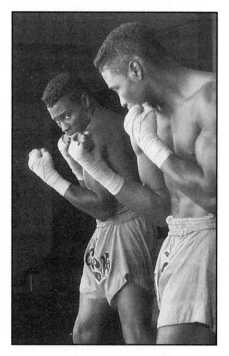

Don't forget that the mirror is made of glass, so exercise caution and maintain a safe distance when working in front of one, especially if you're kicking. And try to keep in mind that you're in front of a mirror to critique your technique, not admire your physique.

SECTION II

WEAPONS

MOVEMENT 7

Something that's often overlooked in kickboxing, or any sport, for that matter, is movement. Virtually everything you will do while training involves some sort of stance or footwork, be it punching, kicking, attacking or defending.

This is a subject that's so simple it often gets complex. There will be times in your training when you'll need to focus on the intricacies of certain movements, while at other times you'll need to think less and just let your body do what it wants to do.

I'll walk you through some basic techniques for moving. The stances and footwork I use are mostly basic boxing techniques, because I find these the most functional methods overall. They have the advantage of having been tested and proven in the ring over decades of boxing competition.

A good kickboxer must learn to move and maneuver with the mindset of working within the confines of a boxing ring. This is necessary whether you intend to compete or if you train for other reasons, since the techniques you'll execute were designed for the ring.

Practice your kicking techniques from a basic boxing stance. You'll need to be able to throw any and all of your kicks from what becomes "your" stance without your opponent or training partner seeing any difference. This cuts down on the chances of "telegraphing" your intentions. But this rule isn't carved in stone. There will be times when you have to make certain adjustments in stances and footwork to deliver certain kicks.

To assume an orthodox (*photo 1*), or left side forward, stance, start with

your feet shoulder width apart. Step forward with your left leg so there is about two feet of depth between your front and back foot, and about eight inches of width. Point the toes of both feet slightly to the right, to what would be between the 12 o'clock and 1 o'clock positions. This stance turns your body slightly to the side, exposing less of your body and fewer targets to your opponent.

Bring both arms up so your fists are about level with your cheekbones, and tuck your elbows in close to the sides of your body. Stand with your knees slightly bent, with a little more of your weight on the balls of your feet than the heels. This is your basic fighting stance.

Are you left-handed? Then you'll use what's called the "southpaw" stance (*photo 2*), which is just the reverse of the orthodox stance, meaning your right side is forward. In the old days, coaches stopped guys from standing with their right foot forward. But if the guy was a southpaw, that was how he'd naturally stand.

You develop your power through your plant foot, so if you're right-handed, you want to plant with your right foot, and if you're left-handed, you want to plant with your left foot. Not exactly rocket science, but very important to your fighting.

Since I'm right-handed, I'll explain these techniques from the orthodox viewpoint. Just one more trial in the plight of lefties.

To move from the basic stance, we'll start with what is called a "step-drag." Pick up your lead foot and step forward, allowing your rear foot to drag forward. It's common to forget about your rear leg to concentrate on what your front foot is doing, but the position of your rear leg and foot are of equal, maybe even greater, importance.

Keep the toes of your rear foot pointed in the same direction as the toes of your front foot, and don't let your rear leg lag behind you. It needs to move in concert with your front leg. To move backward, pick up your rear foot and step to the rear, letting your front foot drag backward.

Practice these movements until they become second nature and you're able to move quickly and efficiently with them without thinking first.

An important point to remember: Do not cross one foot over the other. This type of footwork is common in a variety of martial arts styles, but you will rarely, if ever, see it done by a boxer or kickboxer. It's just too easy to trip over your own feet. Don't do it.

To move sideways, or in a lateral motion, the general rule is you move the leg that's closest to the direction you want to move first. In other words, if you're standing in an orthodox stance and you want to move to your left, move your left (front) leg first, because it's on the same side.

If you want to move to the right from this stance, move your right (rear) leg first. This keeps you from crossing your feet and putting you in a dangerously off-balance position. So the movement to the left is: Step to the side with your lead foot, followed by the right foot stepping in to re-form the original stance. For the right side: Step to the side with your right foot, followed by your left foot.

PIVOTING

Pivoting is a necessary skill, and the hinge to true mobility. It's a simple enough movement that can reap huge benefits, especially in terms of defensive move-ment. A well-executed pivot can not only keep your head on your shoulders where it belongs, it can create openings for your counter-punches or kicks. It also has offensive advantages as well, especially when dealing with someone who's fast on his feet and moves well himself.

To execute a pivot, simply pivot on the ball of your lead foot, dip slightly and place your rear foot behind you. The pivot is usually a 90-degree turn, and you end up in the same stance. The pivot works the same way going to both the left and right, orthodox or southpaw. Remember to keep your hands up in a defensive posture and keep your eyes on your opponent.

Shuffling

Shuffling is another way to move, and adheres to the same basic rules as the step-drag. Its advantage is that it tends to be a quicker movement than the step-drag, and is often used in the ring both to get in close to an opponent quickly, as well as to get away from an opponent quickly. Both are important at different times.

The movement is performed to the front by pushing off with the rear foot and allowing both feet to lightly slide forward along the floor. To withdraw, push off with the front foot and let the feet slide back. To move laterally to the left, push off with your right foot, to move to the right, push with the left.

Your footwork is an area you should strive to master, because if you're going to compete, you're going to get stomped without it. You need the evasive, defensive movement to get you away from your opponent when he's coming at you, and the offensive footwork to get you to your target to deliver the payload.

Some fighters have great footwork, others have sufficient footwork, meaning, it gets the job done. Basic footwork works for everyone straight across the board. But there's more involved footwork, tricks, feinting and faking footwork, that can turn an opponent just for a split second, and that's the second that makes all the difference between him missing a punch and you landing one.

How far you go with your footwork is up to you. I like to dance, and movement is one of my strong points in the ring. They can chase me, but I'm hard to catch. Growing up, I liked to watch Bruce Lee start dancing and picking guys off, and then there was Muhammad "float like a butterfly, sting like a bee" Ali.

These guys were my heroes, and that's what I wanted to do. So when I went to the gym, it was stepping and turning, stepping and turning. I liked that. And since I was already a good dancer, what I wanted to do fit right in with my style. I've never had to think about it much, and I think everyone should give it a whirl.

But everyone isn't me, and we have a lot of different personalities out there. Fighting is a very personal thing. If you just like standing and banging, fine. But you're going to take some shots. You don't have to take it to the extreme that I do, but you will want to master the basics, and then decide what level of showmanship you're comfortable with. Again, the idea is to have some fun.

BOXING&PUNCHES

Before we get into the actual fighting techniques, I want to stress that all of the techniques we'll be teaching, offensive and defensive, are techniques I have used successfully in my training and in the ring. They're not a bunch of textbook practice moves I just think you should learn before moving on to the real stuff; they're the very foundation of my kickboxing skills.

They're also not all the weapons in my arsenal, as I've spent a long time working at this, and much of what I know comes well after the fundamentals stage. But don't feel like I'm short-changing you— there's more than enough here to challenge you for quite some time. Until you've mastered all of the techniques we outline, trying more complex moves is just a waste of your time, and possibly a danger to your health.

These time-tested techniques have been through the long process of trial and error. And not just by me, but by many fighters before me, all of us looking at a wide range of possibilities to maximize their effectiveness. We've weeded out whatever we couldn't get to work in the ring with boxing gloves on, and have left a good, solid skill set for the beginning fighter.

That's not to say these techniques have no self-defense value, that the only place they're effective is in a boxing ring. Just the opposite.

For some reason, martial arts techniques or styles that lean toward actual contact, rather than mastering form, are often disregarded as not being good for self-defense. I've never understood this. Show me a boxer who can throw a jab-right cross combination in the ring and I'll show you someone who'll probably knock out the thug on the street who's giving him trouble. Show me a seasoned judo competitor, wrestler or kickboxer in the same situation and I'll show you a similar result.

Why? It's simple. The *reality* of their training habits. They know a punch, kick, throw or hold works because they've either practiced for competition or trained with people who did. And they're also used to being on the receiving end of things. They have no illusions about what certain techniques can or can't do, and they're no strangers to being hit, kicked, thrown or choked.

This goes back to the possible drawback of traditional martial arts training I mentioned earlier, the occasional unrealistic mindset that can develop when punches and kicks are always pulled and little or no contact is ever made.

Some people become so impressed with how viciously they throw punches and kicks at the air, that they start to think they've got a lightning bolt in one hand, a sledge hammer in the other, and that each leg is a combination jackhammer and bullwhip!

This mindset usually goes hand-in-hand with another, equally dangerous one where the fighter doesn't think much about defense or the reality of taking a hard, well-placed punch or kick. The shock of not knocking your opponent out with your first shot is best learned in the gym, where you'll just be surprised, rather than in the street, where you'll be in big trouble. Taking that first solid hit is also something you don't want to experience in a back alley.

In the gym, your training partner or coach gives you the chance to let the lesson sink in. This gives you the opportunity to realistically assess your skills, and form a suitable strategy for a possible street encounter. A mugger doesn't care about your form or style, and if you've had a taste of competition and know what you can do, you'll have a much better chance of coming out on top.

Realism is particularly important for women to consider when they're choosing a fighting system or if they're already involved in training. Many women train for the purpose of self-defense, and should always keep in mind the real effectiveness of their training. Kickboxing will give you that sense of reality, especially if you compete.

Competition is not a prerequisite for effective technique. The flip side is that I've known a number of traditional martial artists who've never stepped foot into a competitive arena, and seem to possess those lightning bolts, sledge hammers and jackhammer/bullwhips!

Boxing constitutes half of the sport of kickboxing, but it seems to be an area that's often overlooked. It's called kick*boxing* for a reason. In the early days of my career, I often came out on top against fighters who were great kickers, but had no hands to back it up.

My boxing skills were the ace up my sleeve. I've seen many instances where one fighter was an excellent kicker, but the other fighter had better hands. Once the puncher got inside the range of the kicker's legs and it became a close-quarters fight, it was all over. This isn't always the case, of course. Sometimes the kicker is so good, the other fighter can't get close enough to punch. But there seems to be something in the mentality of the "kicker" that often doesn't want to have anything to do with learning to box well or even to defend against it.

My philosophy has always been that I'm going to go to war totally outfitted, with my guns loaded both upstairs and down. If the opportunity to punch presents itself, I'll capitalize on it just as I would if I see an opening to kick. It's as simple as using the right tool for the right job.

In terms of specific boxing techniques, the jab is probably the most basic punch in boxing, and also the most important. It's great to keep your opponent at bay, and also to set him up for other harder techniques. The jab's not necessarily the hardest hitting punch, but it's a good little sticker. Many of the combinations you'll use will be initiated with a jab, and it is also an excellent choice for ending a sequence of punches and kicks, as a way of putting distance between you and your opponent.

A lot of bangers, guys who don't jab, will just walk right up to each other and punch the crap out of each other. They look awful. If you don't jab, you'll take a lot of punishment. A guy who stays away and keeps jabbing will have his glove in his opponent's face every time he comes forward.

Nobody wants to get hit, and it will slow the other guy down and keep him back.

It can be used anywhere—to your opponent's face, his body, as a single punch or multiples in rapid succession. It is a vital punch to develop, and many fighters, myself included, believe that if you develop a good jab you've won half the battle. People argue over which punch is second-most important, but everyone agrees: The jab, she's number one.

To execute a jab, step forward slightly while extending your lead hand forward, turning your fist over so that your palm is facing down. A short

step helps to create momentum behind the punch, but it may not be necessary if your target is within range.

The twisting motion of turning the hand over provides a stinging, cutting effect to the punch that is always handy. If you're shooting for the head, the usual target, aim at your opponent's jaw, nose, or either eye. Be sure to keep your rear hand up to guard your chin and extend your jabbing arm fully. The jab can be thrown while moving forward, backward or from a stationary position. Practice jabbing in singles, in combinations, and while moving in all directions. Mastery of this technique should be a primary goal in your training.

THE RIGHT CROSS

The right cross, sometimes called the straight right, is a power punch and ultimately has one purpose: To knock your opponent out. At the very least, when delivered properly the right cross should get your opponent's attention and his respect. I use it to hurt him as soon as there's an opening, whether he makes a mistake and gives me a shot or I create an opening with my jab.

The right cross can be equally effective to the head and body, and it has a devastating accumulative effect. I've also found this to be an effective counter technique in the ring against kicks, and I often use it when an opponent tries to catch me without setting the kick up with a punch first.

To throw a right cross properly, the arm, shoulder, hip and leg of the punching side must work in unison. As you extend your arm straight forward in a line from your shoulder to your opponent's head, pivot on the ball of your rear foot, allowing your body

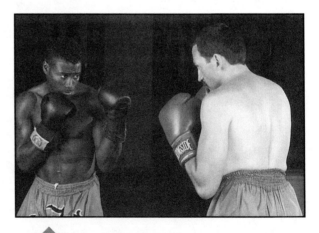

weight to be transferred through your hip, torso, shoulder, arm and ultimately, your hand.

If you didn't pivot, the punch wouldn't reach your opponent, or if it did, wouldn't have enough power to be effective. Keep your other hand up to protect your face, keep your chin tucked next to your shoulder, and at the end of your move you should be able to look down your extended arm as if you were looking down the barrel of a shotgun.

THE HOOK

The hook is a beautiful technique, but hard to master because of the distance involved and the positioning of the arm and body. At the same time, once mastered, this punch is responsible for more knockouts than any other single technique. The hook is effective to the body or head because of the torquing of the punch and the close proximity to the opponent. It packs a lot of wallop for the money, and many fighters use the hook to the body to wear down an opponent.

When throwing a left hook, the arm comes up parallel to the ground as the front foot pivots inward. The pivot puts your weight on that foot and, consequently, behind your punch. As with the other punches, keep your chin tucked out of harm's way, and allow your body to move with the technique. When throwing the hook to the chin or jaw, I aim a little further back to allow for my opponent feinting back to try to evade the punch. Either way, the punch lands.

If I hook to my opponent's head, I turn my palm down as I punch. If I'm going to the body, there are two ways to throw the punch: Thumb up or palm up. Either way is effective and usually dependent on how your opponent is standing and how his guard is positioned. I like to dig the punch in with my palm up if I think my opponent is open to attack in his mid-section. If he is covering well to the front, there may be an opening on either side, and this is when I would try a hook with the thumb up, to attack his kidney areas.

THE UPPERCUT

The uppercut is a punch that seems to be missing from a lot of fighters' arsenals. This punch is nasty when used to an opponent's chin, and is a great set-up for a finishing hook. Like the hook, it's also effective when thrown to the body, and looks very similar in this regard. This punch is very versatile in that it can be thrown to the chin or body with either hand with equal results.

Uppercuts, like hooks, are often one-shot knockouts, as was the case in a match I had with a Muay Thai fighter at Hollywood High School in Los Angeles in the mid-'80s. The Thai hold their hands in a way that works with their kicking style but often leaves them open up the middle. My opponent had ducked under a jab I'd thrown, and stayed crouched long enough for me to come up with an uppercut that landed on his chin and knocked him out cold. Like I said, effective.

To throw the uppercut to your opponent's chin with the lead hand, you must first bob to your left. Once again, you're transferring your weight for purposes of leverage. As soon as your right shoulder dips forward, twist your torso back to its original position while bringing your fist up, palm facing you, to the point of contact under your opponent's chin. This motion should be executed very quickly, and you may be surprised to learn just how close you can be to someone and throw this technique.

To throw the uppercut from the rear hand, use a movement similar to the one used when throwing the right cross, namely the pivot of the back foot and the hip rotation. As you pivot your foot, extend your arm, palm facing you, and shoulder forward to your opponent's chin. Be careful that you don't drop your punching hand as you're starting the movement, as this is a common mistake, and it leaves you open to a left hook counter. Keep your chin tucked and your head slightly to the left of your punch, not directly behind it. Your right shoulder should be ahead of your left shoulder.

To throw an uppercut to the body with the lead hand, bob to the left deeper than you did when punching to the head, and shoot the punch straight up to the opponent's solar plexus with your palm facing you. With the rear hand, step up as you pivot and drive the uppercut into his solar plexus.

THE OVERHAND RIGHT

The overhand right is a variation of the right cross. Whereas with the right cross your punching arm stays aligned with your head, the overhand right follows a slightly curved path to the same target, with a space between your head and your punching arm. This can be an effective way to penetrate the defenses of a skilled fighter that  you're not able to nail with the standard right hand.

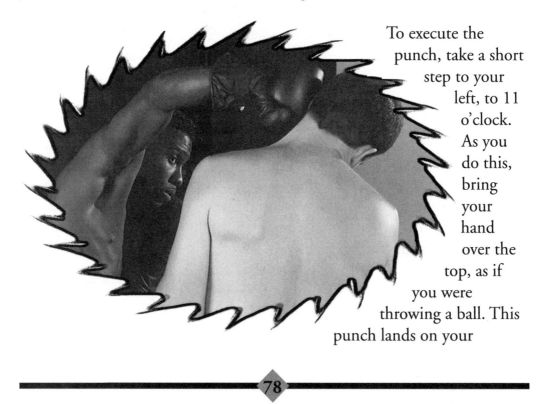 To execute the punch, take a short step to your left, to 11 o'clock. As you do this, bring your hand over the top, as if you were throwing a ball. This punch lands on your

opponent, the knuckles of your fist down, at 12 o'clock. The overhand right is often aimed at the temple, the side of the jaw or the ear, and is good for going around or over your opponent's guard, or a punch he has thrown in a lazy manner.

These punches are the basic building blocks of your boxing attack, half of your kickboxing arsenal. You can use these punches or slight variations of them to launch an offensive in virtually any situation.

Learn them, and practice them until they are second nature, because when the time comes to use them, you'll have other things to think about than how to throw the punches.

FUNDAMENTAL KICKS

My old boxing coach, Ed Couzens, once told me that while it's impossible to throw every technique perfectly and land every technique that you throw, a fighter shouldn't stop trying to achieve this level of skill.

In other words, the quest for perfection should never be abandoned, and this is especially important when it comes to kicking. I see too many fighters who have learned, literally, a couple of kicks and left it at that. This may work for some, but if you spend enough time training and work with enough different people you'll find that certain kicks work on some fighters, but not others.

Humans are such complex animals that you'll inevitably run across people in your training or in competition who come at you from unorthodox angles with unorthodox techniques, and the kicks you'd normally throw don't land or have no effect on them. If you have a wider range of kicks to draw from, you stand a greater chance of being effective against this type of fighter.

In the early days of my training, I spent a lot of time going back to the drawing board, deciding what worked and what didn't, with the goal of trying to make every kick work. Often, it was simply a matter of putting a different twist on an existing technique.

Take the traditional side kick, for instance. Instead of striking with the side of the foot and the edge of the heel, sometimes I'll turn my foot so that I kick with the ball of my foot, sort of like a front kick turned over. This has worked for me when I had trouble getting a standard side kick past an opponent's guard because his forearms were at a right angle to the position of my foot. Rather than abandon this kick, I simply alter how I deliver it slightly.

This is a trick I picked up from Bill "Superfoot" Wallace, a former full-contact world champion who wrote the book on how to be sneaky. Bill would tell me, "You may not be the fastest, you may not be the strongest, but you can damn near be the trickiest."

The bottom line here is that sometimes instead of dropping a kick because you can't make it work, you tailor it a little to get the desired results. And often these "bastardized" techniques work the best.

In my personal style of kicking, I use my front (left) leg much like I do my left hand, keeping in mind a basic rule of fighting which holds that the front leg or hand possesses the speed, while the rear leg or hand delivers the power.

I rely heavily on my front leg kicks, what I call "trick kicks." My first influence in this came from watching the Chinese kung fu movie matinees when I was a kid. Later on, I saw Bill Wallace take his expertise with his one-legged approach to kicking into the ring with great success. That helped get kicking straight in my mind.

Before a match I had with Dennis Crawford, a former Canadian lightweight champion who came out of retirement to fight me after I won the title he previously held, he commented to a reporter that I used a lot of fancy, pretty kicks that, according to him, were just for films and television and don't really work in the ring. I proved they do work: I won the fight.

I'm not the only one that holds this philosophy. There was a full-contact fighter from New York in the '70s and '80s named Paul Vizzio who was a beautiful kicker. He would do kicks in the ring people said couldn't be done, kicks that were normally seen only in demonstrations, and he'd make them work. These techniques take more effort than the more basic kicks to master, but once perfected they're beautiful to watch and you can score knockouts with them.

I use a front kick and a snapping round kick like I would use a jab or an uppercut, both offensively and defensively. I use a switch step-round kick like I would use an uppercut to the body or a hook to the head. Side kicks and hook kicks thrown with the front leg offer me a fast method of delivering a powerful technique.

These kicks all have a couple of key factors in common, namely quickness and versatility. While I have nothing against the more powerful kicks that come from the rear leg, keep in mind that your front leg is closest to your opponent, and consequently it's faster to use both offensively and defensively. The more you "educate" your front leg, the better off you'll be.

A versatile front leg also enables you to more effectively use your rear leg, because kicks from your front leg create openings for you to throw the powerful rear leg shots, just as a good jab creates openings for other punches. The theory is the same: Keep sticking your front leg in his face and stomach and you'll see all kinds of opportunities arise for you to throw that rear leg round kick to your opponent's head or that spinning back kick to his body.

THE FRONT KICK

The term "front kick" generally refers to a kick thrown straight out from your body, usually using the ball of your foot as the striking surface. The term can be a little confusing, however, because the kick can be thrown

with either your front or rear leg, in either a snapping or thrusting motion. For our discussion, the term front kick will apply to a kick being thrown with the front leg, unless otherwise specified.

To perform the kick, raise your forward knee, shifting your weight to your rear leg for balance. As your knee comes up to what we call the chambered position, pull your toes back and flex your foot up to expose the ball of your foot. (Achieving this position may take a bit of practice, and I suggest you practice making light contact on a hard surface before you start throwing this kick hard on a bag or with a partner, to ensure that you're making contact with the correct part of your foot. You'll know if you're not doing it right—it's very painful!) Then snap your leg out to either the level of your opponent's solar plexus or chin, the two primary targets for this kick.

Be sure to snap your leg back to the bent position before setting your foot down, as you don't want to leave your leg out in front of you for your opponent to grab, and you'll be off balance in that position.

From the rear leg, chamber the kick the same way, but as the kick comes forward, extend your hip on the side of the kicking leg so that your kick generates the necessary power.

THE SIDE KICK

The side kick has always been a staple of the karate fighter, but it doesn't seem to be used much in the world of kickboxing these days. I'm not sure why, as the kick can be

both fast and powerful to the head or body, and it can be thrown with either leg. My guess is that this current trend is a by-product of the Muay Thai influence. The Thai don't use the side kick, and many fighters today seem to be adopting Muay Thai techniques and discarding their own.

The Thai kicks, while powerful and brutally efficient, are also simpler, more basic techniques. They're usually easier to learn than some of the more "flamboyant" kicks, such as a snapping side kick to the head, that take a lot of work to become proficient with. However, I find these types of kicks come in handy when everyone else is throwing the same kicks and expecting the same kicks to be thrown at them.

In these situations, I find it useful to deviate from the norm and throw a kick that isn't used as often, such as a side kick or a hook kick. I use the side kick primarily with my front leg, and it's one of the main weapons in my arsenal. This kick is more powerful than a front kick, and I throw it everywhere; to the waist, the solar plexus, the chest and the face.

To execute a side kick, chamber your front leg in the same manner you do for a front kick, except as your knee comes up, pivot the foot of your rear leg so your toes are pointing back and your heel is pointing to the front. This movement turns your hips to the position necessary to allow them to generate sufficient power.

Extend your leg out with your kicking foot parallel to the floor, with the striking area, the side of your foot and the heel, pointing toward your opponent. Stop your kick just short of your leg being fully extended, and quickly pull it back to the chambered position before setting your foot back down. Stopping the kick short prevents you from hyper-extending your knee joint and possibly causing an injury.

If you want to thrust the kick instead of snapping it, simply extend your hips toward the direction of the kick a little more, remembering to bring your leg back quickly so your opponent can't grab it. Due to the body alignment and area of your foot used, even when used in a snapping motion, this is a very strong kick.

If you want to throw a side kick from the rear leg, which I seldom do, bring your rear leg up into chamber like you would for a rear leg front kick, but pivot on your front foot as you extend your kick out. Again, the foot pivot of the leg you're standing on, or the post leg, allows you to generate power from your hips.

THE HOOK KICK

Another kick I don't see being used much in the kickboxing ring is the hook kick. Once mastered, this is a very versatile kick that can knock an opponent out. It's very useful in combination with other snapping kicks, it can be used as a long-range weapon to keep someone away from you, and to the surprise of many, it can be used very effectively when an opponent thinks he's too close to you for you to kick him.

The hook kick is sometimes described as a reverse roundhouse, because the mechanics of the kick are the reverse of a round kick. The striking surface for this kick is the point of your heel, which, if you think about it, is very similar to the head of a hammer. Since the general target area for a hook kick is your opponent's head, and specifically, his jaw or temple, you can see how devastating this kick can be.

To throw a hook kick, chamber your leg like you would for a side kick. As you extend your leg out, position your foot the same way you do for a side kick, only alter the aim slightly.

If your opponent's head is at the 12 o'clock position, extend your foot to the right of your opponent's head, at the 1 o'clock position. Just at the end of the kick's extension, fold your leg back to the chambered position, at 11 o'clock. And guess what? His head was in the way! Voilá! You just hit him with a hook kick.

Keep in mind that since this kick is going to your opponent's head, you'll need to get your kicking foot above his shoulder. The hook kick can also be thrown from the rear leg. Granted, this is a difficult variation to execute, but once mastered you'll possess an effective technique that's seldom seen and, consequently, has the element of surprise to its advantage.

To kick with your rear leg, bring that leg up into the same chambered position, only this time the kick will travel from the 11 o'clock position to the 1 o'clock position.

THE SPINNING BACK KICK

Spinning is an excellent way to generate power for a kick, but there are several key elements that must be present for you to use a spin kick successfully. I highly recommend you get in the habit of setting up a spinning kick with a punch or another kick, as one drawback to any spinning technique is that you momentarily have your back to your opponent and are open to counters.

And always look over your shoulder toward the direction you're kicking. This keeps your target in sight and enables you to abort the technique if your opponent has moved out of range or is coming toward you to smother your kick. And your balance will be even more critical when spinning with a kick, so you must focus on keeping your weight centered over your post leg.

To throw a spinning back kick, take a short step forward and to the right with your left leg. This step realigns your body with your opponent's body in compensation for the spin. Without this step, your kick would most likely be off target, landing on the right side of your opponent's body or missing him altogether. Assuming your opponent is an orthodox fighter and is also standing with his left side forward, the step has put your left leg in line with his left leg,

and your right in line with his right. This position enables you to fire the kick back in a straight line toward your opponent.

As you step, pivot on the balls of both feet simultaneously, look over your right shoulder and extend the kick. After you've kicked, you have the option of continuing forward with other punches or kicks, or planting your kicking foot, stepping forward with your left foot, pivoting, and planting your right foot back to return you to your original stance.

There are two variations of this kick, the difference being the position of your kicking foot. Technically, a spinning back kick has the foot positioned with the toes down and the heel pointing up, with the bottom of the heel as the striking surface. This kick is aimed at your opponent's midsection; either his ribs, solar plexus or lower abdomen.

The other version is more of a spinning side kick, and the kicking foot is parallel to the floor in a side kick position. This can be thrown to the midsection, but you can also throw it to your opponent's chest or head.

Both are devastating techniques, and I wouldn't say one is better than the other. I recommend becoming proficient with both, as you'll have opportunities to use both. The back kick version is great for getting between someone's guard, as the kicking foot slips right through his forearms. The side kick version has the option of going high, and is so powerful that it's extremely difficult to block. I often use one version to set up the other.

For example, I may throw the spinning back kick to my opponent's midsection a few times to get him looking out for this one and, probably, causing him to lower his guard a little to protect himself. As soon as he gets comfortable with this one, I throw the spinning side kick high, usually with good results.

The Round Kick

The round kick, or roundhouse, is the workhorse of the kicking world and my personal favorite. The kick can be used with the front leg or rear, snapping, whipping, with a switch step, as a speed technique or as a power technique. Virtually every martial arts style that kicks has some version of a round kick. To describe and demonstrate the kick, I'll break it down into three categories: snapping, with the front leg; whipping, with the rear leg; and switch step, with the front leg.

I probably use the snapping round kick more often than any other kick. Speed is the primary component of my fighting style, and this kick fits the bill for me perfectly. I can use it moving forward, moving back or standing still. I can throw the kick as a single shot, or in combinations of two or three. I sometimes use it as part of a combination with a side kick or a hook kick with the same leg.

I use the snapping round kick like I use my jab or a long hook, to set my opponent up for other techniques. The kick is a simple one to perform. Bring your lead leg up to the chambered position with your foot pointed down. This exposes the instep of your foot, which is the striking surface of this kick. Snap your leg out at your opponent's head, and quickly retract the kick to chamber before setting your leg down. This retraction of your leg is especially important with this kick, to help retain your balance and enable you to kick more than once.

The whipping round kick is the premier technique of Muay Thai, and it's no surprise they use it more than any other kick. Thrown with the rear leg, the kick has devastating power as well as notable speed. Although it can be aimed at any level, it is generally used to attack the head. The kick requires substantial flexibility, as you must attain enough height to angle the kick *down* toward the head, as opposed to a standard rear leg round kick that travels on a horizontal plane.

One benefit of this angle is that the kick has sufficient power to blast through the guard of whomever you're kicking. Another asset of this kick is if you miss, the whipping motion of the kick spins you back around to your starting position. This is a common occurrence in Muay Thai matches. One fighter misses with his kick, but he spins back into position before his opponent can counter.

To execute the kick, you first need to create some momentum. This can be done by raising your back foot off the floor. As you place it back down, your front foot comes up and takes a short step forward. As soon as your front foot is planted, fire the rear leg out and around at head level. The striking surface you use depends on how close or far away your opponent is, but ideally you'll catch him with the lower to middle area of your shin. The footwork of this kick may seem awkward at first, but after you spend some time practicing the steps the movement actually comes rather quickly.

The switch step-round kick may also feel awkward at

first, but this is a very powerful technique that I highly recommend you add to your repertoire. Once mastered, the kick is very fast as well as powerful, it can be thrown in singles, doubles or triples, and it has the advantage of seldom being used outside of Muay Thai, so consequently it has the element of surprise.

Even the execution of the footwork may distract your opponent, as it is a quick and abrupt movement. The mechanics of the kick in essence turn your front leg into your rear leg, thus enjoying the best of both worlds: the speed of the front leg and the power of the rear leg. While the kick can be used to strike your opponent's legs or head, I personally like to use it against his midsection. This kick to the rib cage will put a man down, and it wreaks havoc against his arms if he has his guard up.

The kick is performed by raising your left leg up and turning it out as you set it behind you. As your leg lands behind you, raise your right foot off the floor and immediately set it back down. As soon as it lands, explode with your rear leg and throw a round kick to the rib cage, with your shin as the striking surface.

This movement is similar to the whipping round kick footwork, and it generates almost as much power. You may want to count the steps to establish a rhythm. The movement should be: one-two-kick. It may help to practice the steps without the kick at first to familiarize yourself with the cadence.

You've now got a strong foundation for a formidable kicking attack. These kicks are just as important as your boxing arsenal, and should be practiced with the same amount of diligence and enthusiasm. You may be tempted to emphasize one over the other in your training, but don't give in—that's how weaknesses are created.

BASIC KNEES AND ELBOWS

Nasty techniques that can't be ignored

Knee and elbow strikes are relatively simple techniques that can be devastatingly effective. Although it is rare to see a kickboxing bout that allows the use of knees and elbows outside of Thailand, they do take place on occasion, and I've fought in bouts where they were allowed. Many people feel these techniques have no place in competition because of the potential for damage and injury they bring to the contest.

While I understand these concerns, I also feel that training, preparation and exposure should be factored in as well. If I agree to a match that includes knees and elbows, I know what to look for and what to expect because I've trained accordingly.

Knees and elbows are excellent weapons for self-defense, so even if you never step foot into a ring or spar, you should practice both the defensive and offensive aspects of using knees and elbows during the course of your training.

Knee and elbow techniques are great equalizers for women in self-defense situations. If you try to punch a thug in the head, you hurt your hand, but if you hit him with an elbow, you hurt his head. And a woman can hit just as hard with the strength in her legs as a man.

A woman can put a male attacker in some serious trouble with her knees, and that's not even necessarily targeting the groin. A good shot to the ribs or stomach will convince most attackers they've picked the wrong victim.

Because of their potential to inflict injury, be careful when practicing your knees and elbows as a beginner. Start by practicing them in front of a mirror, and when you're more comfortable, move on to the heavy bag.

Even as you become more experienced, be very cautious when using knees and elbows with a partner. Elbows are particularly dangerous, as most of the strikes are designed to go to the head, and even a little touch can cut someone. That's why they're so effective for self-defense.

THE KNEE

There are two methods of striking with your knee, the straight, or inside knee, and the side, or outside knee. The straight knee could best be described as a stubby front kick, because the knee is thrown the same way you do your front kick. The most important thing to remember when using the knee is to drive your knee forward, not up. If the knee travels up, it will only graze your target, as opposed to driving forward and through it.

The knee is generally thrown from the rear leg to produce the maximum power. Simply bring your rear leg up as if you were doing a front kick with the rear leg, only leave your leg bent in the chambered position and drive your hips forward, striking with the point of your knee to your opponent's midsection. Imagine your knee is a battering ram; this may help you drive it forward.

You can also drive your knee straight into the front of your opponent's thigh. This is a nasty little technique that can cause the muscles in the front of his leg to cramp up, affecting his ability to kick or knee with that leg effectively.

The outside knee gets its name from how it is delivered; the knee is brought out to the side of the body and then pulled in to the opponent's floating ribs, using the inside of the knee joint as the striking surface.

This technique is very effective in close, and is often used in Muay Thai matches. This type of knee works best when used in conjunction with a headlock. In this method, the hips generate the power behind the strike as they work in concert with the headlock.

To practice the technique from an orthodox stance, grasp your partner around the neck with your left hand grabbing your right wrist, and pull his head toward you, keeping your elbows as close together as possible. In essence, you're making a vise with your forearms. Raise your right knee out to the 3 o'clock position, and pull him toward your knee as you bring your knee down and into his side.

You can use your front knee as well. This version entails using a short hop to the left with your right foot as you bring your left knee out to the 9 o'clock position. As with the first method, pull your opponent toward your knee as you bring it in and down.

You can also use the headlock to move your opponent into position for the knee strike, or just to control him. A word of caution, though: **Always be careful when practicing or using any technique that involves someone's neck, because of the serious ramifications should an injury occur to this area.**

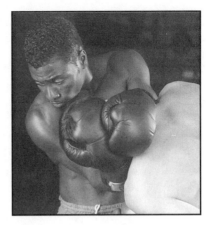

Once you've secured the headlock, if you want to move your opponent to the right, take your left hand and push his head in that direction as your right wrist applies pressure to the left. Then step out with your right foot and pull him around. To move him to the left, push his head with your right hand and step out with your left. The leverage you're able to generate with this technique may surprise you, so again, be careful when using it.

THE ELBOW

Most styles of martial arts utilize elbow strikes, and kickboxing is no exception. But I think the elbows used in kickboxing are a bit more creative, which makes them more effective. An elbow strike is obviously used for close quarters combat, and a good shot with your elbow is often the best choice in a self-defense situation. All of the elbow strikes we'll cover are used to the front, but the difference is the angles with which they are thrown.

Elbows are thrown in a very simple manner, using the

bony point as the striking surface. The first striking technique is a horizontal elbow, which can be thrown from the front or rear. Using your left, bring your arm around like you are throwing a hook, only keep your arm bent and your fist right in front of your face. Pivot if necessary on your front foot, and strike your opponent right across his jaw.

From the rear, your right arm comes across to the point of your opponent's jaw. Remember to allow your hips and rear leg to pivot and generate power like they do when you throw a right cross.

The vertical elbow resembles an uppercut. To throw the left, raise your elbow so your fist passes on the outside of your head and the point of your elbow comes up under the point of your opponent's chin and drives up. The right elbow is thrown the same way as the left. Both of these are effective for coming between someone's guard.

The third version is the diagonal elbow, which is not as common as the others, but arguably the most effective of the three. This is more of a cutting technique, and the target area follows a line from above the eye down across the bridge of the nose. It is very effective for coming over your opponent's guard, and this technique fits quite nicely into the "sneaky" category.

To throw this elbow with either arm, keep your fist in place while you rotate your elbow up above either side of your opponent's head, then drop it down and across his face. The motion is similar to that of the overhand right. To add more power to this technique, simply pick up the foot that's on the same side as the elbow you're going to use, and set it down as your elbow comes down.

Again, these are very effective techniques for equalizing an attacker on the street or for high-level competition, and have a definite place in your training. But please keep in mind while practicing them their tremendous potential for harm, and never allow yourself to get careless and injure your coach or your training partner. It's hard to forgive and forget a good knee or elbow strike.

SECTION III

DEFENSE

DEFENSIVE MOVEMENT

The easiest way to win a fight, whether in the ring or on the street, is to not allow your opponent to hit you. In the ring, of course, you'll have to land some of your own, but on the street, just not getting hit when someone comes after you is a victory. If he can't hit you, he can't hurt you.

That doesn't mean you'll never get hit. As I've said, you will, and that's not necessarily a bad thing, if you're getting hit in practice. I think it's beneficial to condition your body to take some punishment, as your body is capable of adapting to impact to a certain degree.

Also, much of our ability to deal with getting hit is psychological, and we often think we're hurt worse than we really are. But while I feel it's important to be able to take a shot if one gets through, I'd rather see you learn to block and evade attacks skillfully.

Learning how to move the upper body and head is an important aspect of defense for even the casual participant, and an absolute must for the competitor. The basic movements are bobbing, weaving and feinting. These are designed primarily to move your head out of the way of punches.

Bobbing, sometimes called slipping, is used as a defense against a jab coming straight towards your face. Weaving is used primarily to get out of the way of a hook or a cross. Feinting can be used both offensively and defensively, to fake your opponent and throw off his timing, or to evade jabs, uppercuts and high snapping kicks.

All three are very simple movements and are among the most basic of fighting skills, and the time you spend mastering them will be repaid in the bruises you don't get from your opponents.

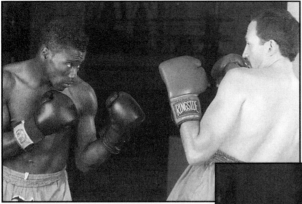

BOBBING

Bobbing is performed by bending at the waist, putting the weight on the forward leg as you twist your torso so your rear shoulder is now in

front. If you're bobbing to the right, your head moves from a 12 o'clock position to a 1 o'clock position.

Bobbing to the left moves your head to an 11 o'clock position. Imagine that your head moves along the lines of an inverted "v" when bobbing to the left and right. Bobbing will gain a new significance as you start incorporating it into countering a little later on.

WEAVING

Weaving is used to evade any type of swinging punch coming at the side of your head. If you tried bobbing with these types of punches you would get hit anyway, because your head is on the same plane as the punch, so you need to take your head out of the path of the incoming attack.

To weave, bend your legs to drop you out of the path of the punch, then move your

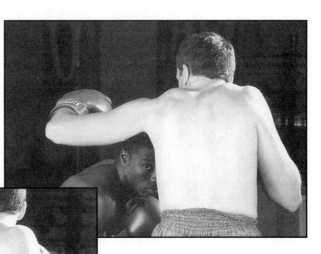

head in the direction the punch came from. Imagine making a "u" with your head; your head actually

ends up behind the punch that was thrown. This presents you with some excellent countering opportunities, which we'll also explore later.

FEINTING

To feint defensively, step back a few inches with the rear foot only and pull your head and torso out of the way, then replace your rear foot. This movement, when viewed from the side, resembles a cobra preparing to strike, and it can be equally effective.

To use a feint offensively you want your opponent to think that you're moving forward when you're not. You can do this to test his reactions, helping you plan your strategy. To feint forward, either take a short step or act like you're taking a step and exaggerate your shoulder movement.

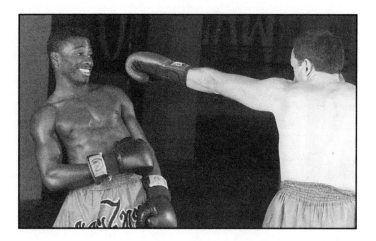

These techniques are very effective in keeping you from getting hit, and frustrating your opponent. If you can make him miss a few times, he may call off the attack. He may lose his cool and lose his fighting mind, and then you've got him. So maybe the old saying's right, the best offense is a good defense.

BOXING 12 DEFENSES

Minimizing the damage

Evasive movement won't always get you out of the way of an attack, and sometimes you don't want it to. But you don't want to give your opponent a free shot either, which is where parrying and blocking come into play.

PARRYING

Parrying is a subtle yet extremely effective way of redirecting a punch, such as a jab or right cross, that's coming straight at your face.

From an orthodox stance the parry is usually done with the right hand, but the left could be used as well. As the punch comes toward you, open your hand inside your boxing glove, so your glove resembles a catcher's mitt. Don't reach out for the punch, but rather intercept it by moving your glove across your face.

You only need to move the punch the width of your face, roughly cheekbone to cheekbone, because you must bring your hand back to the on-guard position

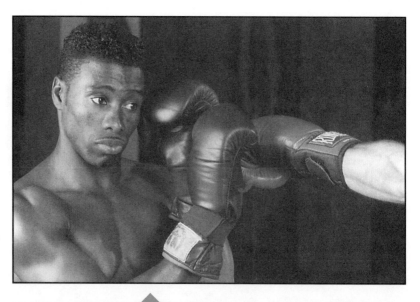

immediately. Keep in mind that it isn't necessary for you to evade punches or kicks by a huge margin, just enough for them to miss. If a technique only missed you by an inch, it still missed you.

If you move too far away, you're out of range to counter with a punch or kick of your own. You should get in the habit of punching off of your parry. One example of this would be after parrying a jab with your right hand, you counter with a jab of your own. Another would be to parry with your right hand and immediately throw a straight right at your opponent while his arm is extended.

BLOCKING

Sometimes you won't be able to bob, weave, feint or parry fast enough to avoid getting hit and you'll have to block the punch. This block isn't much more than covering up so the punch doesn't do any real damage, but there's still a correct way to do it.

As the punch comes in, tuck your chin into your chest and turn your face slightly away from the punch. If you leave your chin up you're liable to get hit by your own glove when your opponent's punch hits it.
This is not only dangerous, it's embarrassing as well!

Your elbow and arm should be tight against your body for protection, and you absorb the punch on your glove. Some fighters bend their wrist up slightly, which in effect makes a bump on the back of their wrist that serves to deflect the force of the punch.

A smart fighter that has good boxing skills will invariably attack your body, and it's imperative that you know how to defend against this. You don't want someone using your rib cage for a substitute heavy bag.

To prevent this, use your forearm and your elbow to protect each side of your torso. Keep your chin tucked as the punch comes in, and turn in slightly so the punch lands on your arm. Your arm should be snug against your body. If it's not, your opponent's punch will knock your arm into your side, and it's liable to hurt as much as his punch would have.

There is one situation that may require you to use a combination of a parry and a block, and that's when defending against an uppercut to the chin. I suggest you use your rear hand for this block, although you could use either, depending on which hand your opponent was using to punch.

The block is performed by opening your glove like you would to parry, and then turning it over and pushing down slightly as the upper-cut comes up towards your chin. The idea  is to catch the punch in your glove firmly enough to stop its upward motion.

Don't reach for this punch, either, as this will put your hand too far away from you, and could get you in trouble. If your hand's too far away, it will take too long for you to bring it back to the guard position, and in the meantime you're open to attack.

Practice these techniques until they're reactions. You should automatically know when to block and when to parry, as your opponent isn't likely to give you time to decide.

KICKING DEFENSES

When you consider how powerful kicks can be, the importance of properly blocking or avoiding them becomes readily apparent. As with punches, it's best if you can avoid or redirect when someone kicks at you, but this isn't always possible. Sometimes contact is inevitable, but there are a number of ways to effectively deal with these situations, such as the leg check, redirection and the reinforced block.

As I mentioned earlier, the one technique that sets kickboxing apart from other forms of competitive martial arts is probably the use of kicks to the legs, or leg kicks. As effective as this technique is, there are ways to block it and avoid it.

THE LEG CHECK

The most common method is called the leg check, or simply, the check. This involves using your shin to stop the kick before it gets to your thigh or calf. Okay, okay, I know what you're thinking—ouch! This Cunningham guy is nuts!

Granted, the thought of banging shins with your opponent is not most people's idea of a good time, but it's not quite as bad as it sounds. And bare shins are generally only seen in competition, so many of you will avoid this sensation altogether.

While you're training, you usually wear shin pads when sparring or doing drill work with another person. These pads absorb some of the impact and help prevent injuries. They also let you gradually toughen up your shins, since some impact can be still felt through the padding.

This may still sound a little brutal, but remember that the leg check can be used to protect both the outside and the inside of your thighs or calves, and trust me, once you've taken a solid shot to the thigh, you're liable to think checking isn't such a bad idea.

To check to the outside, (the most common target for a leg kick is the front thigh) raise your front leg up and point your knee out at a 45-degree angle. Remember to keep your hands up to protect your head, and bend your post knee slightly.

Some fighters point their checking foot down, but I prefer to bend my foot up. I feel this keeps my opponent's kicking leg from sliding down my shin and smacking my post leg, which some fighters do intentionally to sweep their opponents off their feet. If someone attempts to kick your rear leg, the check is the same on that side.

Occasionally, someone may try to kick the inside of your front thigh. This may come from the southpaw fighter's rear leg, or an orthodox fighter using a switch step kick with his front leg. Either way, the defense is the same. Simply raise your front leg and point your knee slightly to your right, checking the kick.

REDIRECTION

A thrusting front kick with either leg contains a lot of force, and I suggest you avoid checking or blocking them if possible. When an opponent kicks to your midsection with a straight technique, usually a front kick, the best defense is redirecting.

The purpose of redirecting is to move your opponent's attacking leg away from you while staying close enough to hit him with a counter. The movement is something of a combination of feinting back with your hips and parrying with your forearm, and it reminds me of the way a matador moves in a bullfight.

As a rule, if your opponent's in the same stance you are and he kicks with his left (front) leg, you redirect with your left arm. If he kicks with his right, you'll redirect with your right.

To execute the technique, as a front kick comes in from your opponent's lead leg, step back and pull your hips out of the way as you move slightly to the right. At the same time you're moving, turn your left arm down at the elbow, scooping the kick to the left with your forearm or, sometimes, your boxing glove.

Your body should be just outside of the path of the kick, which keeps you from being kicked if the movement doesn't work for some reason. If the kick comes from the right (rear), reverse the

motion—step back and to the left as you parry the kick to the right. As you practice redirecting, always visualize what types of punches and kicks you could counter with, which helps puts the movement into context.

Keep in mind that these defenses are simply one link in a chain of movements. All of these actions will be followed—and quickly—by another, so don't get so comfortable with any one movement that you think performing it properly is the end. It's just the next step.

No matter how good you get at leg checking and redirecting, eventually you're not going to be able to stop someone from getting a kick through. I've said it all along—you're going to get hit, it's inevitable. But that doesn't mean you have to stand there and take it.

THE REINFORCED BLOCK

A reinforced block is an effective way to avoid taking the full blast of your opponent's attack.

The reinforced block requires you to re-educate your body a little. Usually, our natural reaction when we're being hit is to turn away from the direction of the assault. Many times this is the worst thing you can do. With this block, you're going to turn into the attack and meet it head on.

You generally use this block against a power kick to your body, like a rear leg round kick or a spinning back kick. As the kick comes in, turn your upper body at the waist toward the kick and bring your forearms together, snugly against your body.

Your forearms will take the brunt of the kick. This may sting a little, but it's much better than taking the kick in the ribs. This technique works the same on either side of your body, and in both cases your hands are in a good position to counter with a punch.

ARM AND LEG BLOCK

Another block is a more traditional Muay Thai block, and it involves using your arm and leg. The logic here is you can see a kick coming toward you, but you're not sure where it's going to land, so you use this block because it covers the entire side of your body.

To use this one, bring the leg of the side you're blocking with up and point your knee out to the side at either the 10 o'clock or 2 o'clock position. Position your same-side arm directly above your leg, with your arm bent out at a 45-degree angle.

There should be little or no space between your arm and the top of your raised leg. Keep your post leg bent slightly at the knee to accommodate the force of the incoming kick. This block also works on both sides of your body.

HIP FEINT

If you would rather evade the leg kick altogether than check it or block it, you can do what's called feinting back with the hips. This movement can be also be used to avoid a front kick. The basic premise is you remove the target from the range of the attacking weapon. In other words, your opponent can't hit what's not there.

This is a simple, effective movement that has the advantage of being extremely frustrating to your opponent. When done properly, it appears as if you haven't moved, and your opponent feels like he's kicking at a ghost.

Other advantages are you don't get hit, which reduces the possibility of injury, and you can counter quickly because of the short distance between you and your opponent.

To feint back with your hips effectively you must master the timing of the movement. Feint too soon, and your opponent knows what you're up to. Feint too late, and you get hit. As the kick comes in, take a small step back with your rear leg,  pull your hips back and let your front foot slide back momentarily.

Immediately after the kick has missed, take a short step forward and reestablish your original stance. Your upper body shouldn't move or change position; the movement here is all from the waist down. Practicing this technique with a mirror to the side of you will enable you to see the motion of your hips. Work on this until it becomes something you can do quickly and smoothly, remembering that each time you do it right is one less time you get hit.

Just as you learned how devastating your leg kicks can be to your opponent, you need to remember his leg kicks have the same potential for damage to you. Mastering these techniques will help you keep your opponent from reaching his potential, and significantly reduce your bumps and bruises.

KNEE AND ELBOW DEFENSES

16

Not getting bludgeoned

As devastating as knee and elbow strikes can be, there are very effective ways to protect yourself against them. As we discussed, knees to the body are usually done with a headlock. If you find your head in the middle of one of these and you see a knee zooming in, you have several defensive options, but you'll want to choose quickly.

KNEE DEFENSES

The first is a simple block, where you cross your forearms in front of your body to prevent your opponent's knee from making contact with your torso. Try to position your arms so that when his knee comes up the top of his thigh

hits the point of your elbow. This may slow him down a little, but the situation still pits his knees against your arms, and he's liable to win this contest.

A more effective strategy would be to parry the knee around and sweep his post leg. You want to redirect his leg to the outside, so if he knees with his right leg, use your right arm to scoop under his leg, reach behind him with your left hand and grab his shoulder / neck area, and sweep his post leg with your left foot.

If he knees with his left, scoop with your left arm and sweep with your right. This is a very slick technique, and it has the feeling of turning the hunter into the hunted. One minute your opponent has you in a headlock and is about to knee your guts into hamburger, and in a split second he's on his back on the floor at your mercy.

When you're practicing this technique, make sure that you control your partner's fall so he isn't injured.

Probably the simplest way to guard against the knee strike is to prevent your opponent from being able to throw it in the first place. This is done by grabbing him around the waist as soon as he gets you in the headlock, and pulling his body next to yours.

Done properly, this disrupts his balance and he loses his leverage. There's no knee happening from this position, but you are in a great position to hook one of your legs behind one of his, dropping him to the floor.

REVERSING THE HEADLOCK

As you've probably noticed, the headlock is an important part of the knee scenario. While it's a very strong hold, it's not invincible, and if you find yourself on the receiving end of one, there is a way to get out of it. Even better, in getting out of it, you reverse it, and your

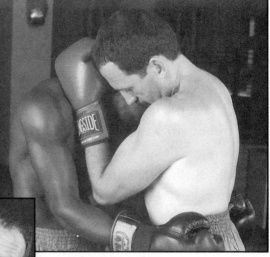

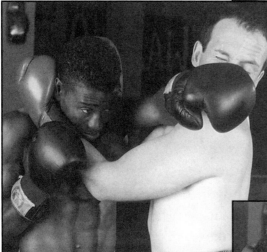

opponent ends up in your headlock.

Starting from the position of being in a headlock, make a

knife hand with your left hand and wedge it between your head and your opponent's head. Using your hand, wrist and forearm, drive his head and neck back. This creates space between you and loosens his grip.

At this point, reach up through the middle with your right hand and grab him behind his head and neck and pull down. Immediately, withdraw your left arm and reach up the middle with it, securing a grip behind his head and neck with your left hand. You've now reversed the hold, and hopefully he doesn't know this technique.

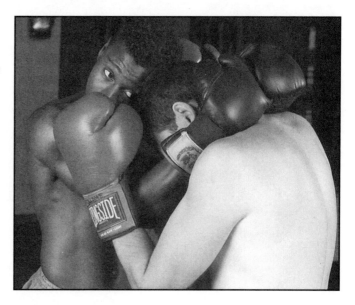

ELBOW DEFENSES

To defend against an elbow attack, you'll want to either stay out of range so you can't be reached with an elbow strike, tie your opponent up with a head-lock so he can't throw

one, or use a modified boxing block, taking the elbow on your gloves. Again, when using the modified boxing block, be sure there's no room between you and your gloves, or your opponent will knock you silly with your own gloves. Not a pretty picture.

SECTION IV

COMBOS AND COUNTERS

BOXING COMBINATIONS

Knowing how to perform individual boxing punches is not a sufficient level of skill for a kickboxer. The name of the game, whether punching, kicking or both, is combinations. My boxing skills have always been one of my strong points, and my ability to deliver a variety of combinations is a big part of that effectiveness.

Now we'll cover some basic combinations I think should be added to your bag of tricks. I'll focus on the punches and kicks separately before we combine the two later on. This is especially important if you already have a kicking background, because your natural tendency may be to focus on the kicking techniques and somewhat ignore the punches. As I've stressed, both are of equal importance, and by initially focusing on them separately, you have a better chance of making them work together later.

JAB-RIGHT CROSS

A fighter's repertoire would be incomplete without the classic combination of the jab-right cross, or straight right, which is often referred to as "the old one-two." Some techniques, no matter how basic or well-known, just seem to stand the test of time, and this combo is one of them.

This duo is what I call a "building block"; used properly, the jab-right cross will initiate much of your offensive work, whether it's punches only or punches and kicks.

To throw the jab-right cross, I like to take a short step forward as I jab. This helps bridge the gap between my opponent and myself, and it puts me a little closer for that powerful right hand that's coming next.

Make sure you rotate your jabbing hand all the way over before starting the right cross, and keep your right hand up, with your fist protecting the side of your head.

It's a common mistake to get in such a hurry to get to the second or third technique in a sequence that the initial technique is a bit sloppy. Since each part of a combination builds on the parts before it, you want each technique to be sharp.

After you've fully extended the jab and you're retracting your arm, the right should be on its way out. Timing here is crucial: Throw your right too soon and you've opened the right side of your head to attack, throw it too late and your opponent has

probably reacted to the jab, moved, and is no longer in range to hit.

As your right arm extends, bring your left hand back to protect that side of your head. And perhaps most importantly, let your right foot pivot so your hips can transfer power to your punch.

Not surprisingly, after "the old one-two" comes "the old one-two-three." This is the last technique that will be numbered; a lot of fighters can't count any higher than this.

The jab-right cross-left hook to the head is another very basic, very effective combo. I like it because after throwing two straight shots at your opponent, you change the angle dramatically and attack from the side.

The hook is the punch that accounts for a lot of the "mystery" knockouts in boxing. This is the situation where one fighter goes down, apparently for no reason, and the "experts" in the crowd yell, "Fix!" Not hardly. This punch is deceptively powerful, especially when expertly placed on the point of the chin or the side of the jaw.

When throwing this combination, it helps to feel the rhythm as your arms work in concert. Working your punches in combinations should have

something of a push-pull feel to it. In other words, you jab, then as you push your right out you pull your jab back, and as you pull your right back you come across with your hook.

The three work off of each other, and regardless of the speed with which they're thrown, a definite tempo should be established. And like the old man in the movie *The Karate Kid* said, "Don't forget to breathe—very important!"

The most common error I see when people use this trio is they tend to drop their right hand when they bring it back, which leaves them open for the same left hook they're about to throw. And when throwing that hook, make sure you allow your front foot to pivot inward as the punch comes over. Again, this pivot allows your hips to transfer power to the punch.

A jab-right cross-left hook to the body is another workhorse technique that has a prominent place in the arsenal of many of the best fighters. Many boxers consider this a "bread and butter" technique, one that much of their strategy is built around.

World champion Julio Cesar Chavez of Mexico comes to mind as someone who utilizes the hook to the body with brutal effectiveness, banking on the old boxing adage, "Take their body, and their head will follow."

This sequence could be used effectively after your opponent got used to your jab-right cross combo. There's a good chance he'll start over-protecting his head and chin if you've been banging him with your right, and this is liable to cause his guard to be higher than it needs to be, exposing his rib cage.

There's your opening to throw the jab and the right before torquing in a powerful hook to his body. Watch enough boxing matches and you'll see fights won due to one fighter's inability to continue the match after taking too many shots to the body.

JAB-RIGHT CROSS-LEFT HOOK-LEFT HOOK

Next is the jab-right cross-left hook (to the body)-left hook (to the jaw). If you'll notice, there's a definite pattern we're following here, one that naturally progresses and builds upon itself, sort of like building a brick wall. The more bricks you add, the bigger your wall becomes and the stronger it gets. Also notice that we are now changing the levels of the areas that we attack within a given sequence. This, and increasing the number of shots you throw within a combination, are prerequisites to attaining higher levels of skill.

After you have thrown the jab, right cross and hook to the body, you'll go "upstairs" with a left hook to the jaw for two reasons, one mental and one physical. After attacking his body, his mental focus is on that area regardless of the degree of effectiveness the punch had, simply because there was contact there.

And if the punch got through, his physical focus is on that area because of the pain involved and the fear or anticipation of more to come to the same area. Plus, your opponent will have a natural tendency to drop his guard to cover his rib cage, and this will expose his jaw, creating an opening for your hook.

When executing the technique, you should feel that push-pull rhythm again when withdrawing from your body shot in preparation for the hook to the head, and remember to allow your front foot to pivot inward as you throw the hook.

JAB-RIGHT CROSS-LEFT HOOK-RIGHT CROSS

Next up is the jab-right cross-left hook (to the body)-right cross (to the jaw) sequence. Now you're really beginning to build upon the foundation you've established by working on these techniques individually. This combination, with its four components, is likely to confuse your opponent, who is probably only expecting two or, maybe, three punches at a time.

You go through your basic jab-right cross-left hook, but add on another right cross at the end of your sequence. The left hook should encourage your opponent to let his guard down around his face, giving a perfect opening for a finishing right cross to his jaw. Again, be sure to withdraw your punches to their original guard positions. In this case, the tendency may be to drop your left after the hook and prior to the right. This would leave you open to a counter right, a knockout punch, which puts a nasty end to your combination sequence.

As you progress in your training, get into the habit of throwing combos with four, five and six punches and/or kicks. This not only increases your fluidity and expands your personal arsenal, it increases your likelihood of landing the shots.

This is especially important when fighting an experienced opponent or training with an advanced student. You simply won't be able to tag these people with single shots, or even doubles or triples. You may find you have to throw four, five or six to connect with one or two.

Also, get in the habit of finishing each sequence with a jab. This keeps your opponent at bay, what's sometimes called "keeping him honest." A good fighter will retaliate as soon as he senses you're through firing; a finishing jab makes him think twice before countering.

DOUBLE JAB-RIGHT CROSS

A combination I find quite effective is the double jab-right

cross. The difference between someone having a good jab and someone having a great jab is often a matter of not only being able to throw it quickly and accurately, but also in rapid succession. Think of your jab as

a piston; educate your arm so your jab almost seems to fire itself at will.

With the double jab, the first one is thrown to make your opponent react and, hopefully, to make him

reach. The second jab creates a gap that enables you to throw your right cross straight down the pike to the point of his chin. It's common to drop your left hand after the second jab, so be conscious of this and make a mental note that your guard stays up after both jabs.

LEAD RIGHT CROSS-LEFT HOOK

The lead right cross-left hook is the standard, most effective combination to use against a southpaw opponent. When someone faces you with their right side forward, it's difficult to use your jab effectively, because the southpaw's right hand is in front of your left hand, and one nullifies the other.

However, the left side of the southpaw's body and head are open to attack

from your right hand, so it's wise to exploit this opening. The stance of your opponent also puts his chin closer to your left hook; again, here is an opening to be exploited. If the situation calls for it, you may want to step in when you throw the right, backing your opponent up before you come over his right hand with your left hook.

This simple combination, while proven to be effective time and time again against the left-handed fighter, doesn't seem to be used very often by orthodox fighters. They often seem intent on throwing their jab like they always do, and can't figure out why it's not working.

I think the average southpaw isn't on the receiving end of the straight right-left hook combo often enough to develop a solid defense against it, which is another reason to use it.

Another tip when working with a southpaw is to try to keep your front foot to the outside of your opponent's front foot. This should help your balance and put you in a better position to work from.

JAB-RIGHT CROSS-LEFT UPPERCUT

The jab-right cross-left uppercut to the chin comes in handy if your opponent has gotten wise to the jab-right cross-left hook. With virtually no noticeable difference in your stance or demeanor, you can follow the jab and right cross with an uppercut to your opponent's chin, and there's a good chance he won't see it coming.

I like to throw the jab-right cross-left hook combo a few times to get my opponent to expect the hook, then throw everything the same, but substitute the uppercut. This is usually effective, but don't alter your jab in any way or lower that arm in anticipation of throwing the uppercut, as this could alert a crafty opponent that you're up to something.

JAB-UPPERCUT-LEFT HOOK

With a jab-uppercut-hook combination we're attacking all upper level targets, but relying on basic reactions to the punches to assist us. The initial punch, the jab, should cause your opponent to raise his hands to protect himself, and he may look down and tuck his chin as well.

Your uppercut takes advantage of this position and comes up between his arms to his chin. Now you're ready to throw the hook. Why the left hook to finish him off? Normally, his guard may be up well enough to prevent your throwing a successful hook, but the uppercut should pop his head up and out of the protection of his guard, giving you a great opening to finish him off.

ADVANCED JAB-RIGHT CROSS-LEFT HOOK

If there's something today's kickboxer could learn from a traditional martial artist, it's that the solar plexus is still as good a target area as it ever was. The solar plexus is the area of your torso above your abdominal muscles and below your sternum, between the two sides of your rib cage.

This spot is inherently weak on all of us, and it's always been a primary target of most martial arts styles, often the recipient of the classic reverse punch. For some reason, I don't see too many kickboxers attacking this area with anything other than a front kick. A well-thrown straight right, a right cross to the body, is tailor-made for this target area; the technique can be delivered quickly because it's a simple, straight punch, and it travels a relatively short distance from the chambered position to the target.

While you could throw the punch by itself, I like to start with a strong jab to my opponent's face to distract him and bring his guard up. Then I fire the right straight in to his solar plexus, which should cause him to drop his guard. This exposes his head, and he's now open for a finishing hook to the head or jaw.

Your ability to put the basic punches you've already learned together to create these powerful combinations will have a tremendous effect not only on your success in competition, but on your chances of defending yourself on the street. Spend the time to get these down cold, and you'll be well on your way to the next level.

BOXING 16 COUNTERS

If I had to put myself in a category as to what "type" of fighter I am, I'd probably classify myself as a defensive fighter. I'm not saying I feel this is a better style, or I'm never an aggressive fighter. I've had my share of fights that were real slugfests, and I'm not afraid to take the fight to my opponent.

But sometimes I see fighters who focus so heavily on offense and pursuing their opponent that they totally neglect their defensive skills. You may have seen some of these fighters before. You can usually pick them out by their misshapen noses, scars and cauliflower ears. And while being able to take a shot comes in handy, the point of this game is not to see who can take the best beating. I've yet to see a kickboxing match that awarded points for being the ugliest fighter, unlike, say, pro wrestling.

My old sensei, Bob Supeen, Jr., probably said it best. Early in my kickboxing career I had a bout with a fighter that had just switched over from boxing. He'd had a successful amateur career, with maybe as many as 100 or more bouts. And every bout seemed to be right there on his face. This guy had taken some punches, and I was thinking, "Man, he can take some, I'm going to have to be busy."

Sensei Bob saw me staring at Igor's scarred mug, and said, "Don't worry about this guy's face. Worry about the guys who made him that ugly." I ended up knocking him out, his corner threw in the towel. But I did it with my kicking.

You think I'm going to try to work in close with an excellent boxer? You're crazy if you do. I'm going to kick those guys, use my jab to keep them away and crank them with round kicks. I'm not going to let the macho thing get to me. I keep thinking about what Sensei Bob said, and that if someone's going to get ugly, it's not going to be me.

The point, obviously, is there's no rule that says you have to get hit, and I've had a pretty successful career getting my opponents to chase me around the ring, trying to land that one big shot to put me away. Meanwhile, I've been moving, bobbing, weaving, pivoting, slipping, feinting, dancing and evading them, hitting them with my punches and kicks in the process.

My natural attributes are speed and quickness, and these qualities lend themselves to the types of movement necessary to be able to evade punches and kicks. They have also allowed me to create my own style of attacking while on the move. This wasn't anything that was planned; rather, my body type and physical traits set the course for me.

But being able to avoid being hit is not enough to be a successful kick-boxer. Evading your opponent's attacks is one thing, countering with attacks of your own is another. With that in mind, let's examine some punching techniques that I like to use when I'm on the receiving end of things.

COUNTERING THE JAB

First we'll work on counters to the jab. On all but one of these counters, I rely on a bobbing motion to move my face and head out of the path of my opponent's jab. I'm a firm believer in using the right tool for the right job, and with the possible exception of a feint, nothing comes close to a bob to evade a jab. The movement is simple, economical and quick.

As your opponent or training partner jabs to your face, bob to the left and, as your head and torso are

coming back to their original position, fire a jab of your own. This is a situation where the less you think, the better off you'll be, because these movements are happening too fast to allow you the luxury of thinking about what to do.

You must react to what your opponent does, and this only happens after lots of practice in the gym. Often when a fighter has a good jab, he's not used to getting it back, so don't be intimidated by a fast jab. Instead, show him how fast yours is.

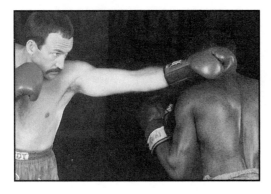

Bobbing to the right this time, you'll throw an overhand right cross to your opponent's jaw. I recommend the overhand version of the right cross because you may find your opponent's punching arm is in the way, preventing you from throwing a standard right cross. If this is the case, you can use your opponent's extended arm as a guide for your counterpunch by throwing your overhand right just above his arm. If you follow his arm all the way down, you'll find his chin at the end, the pot of gold at the end of the rainbow.

You may decide to counter to your opponent's body, rather than his head, when defending against a jab. A hook works well in this situation, regardless of which way you bob to avoid the jab, because the bobbing motion starts the movement and body position you need to throw the hook to the body. When you bob to the left and throw a left hook, watch that you keep your right hand up to protect your face and head, as you're open for a left hook if you don't. Likewise, when you bob to the right and throw a right hook, keep your left hand up for protection, because you're in a position to get nailed if your opponent drops his right hand on you.

Instead of bobbing to evade a jab, you may opt to use a feinting movement, in this case what we call a feint back. This, like the bob, is a very fast method of moving your head out of the way of a jab. The most noticeable difference between the two

is that with the feint your head goes back in a straight line, as opposed to a

bob going forward at one of two angles. As I mentioned earlier, a feint back resembles a cobra preparing to strike. The feint and right cross work well together as a counter because the backwards motion of the feint generates power that can be transferred with the forward motion of the feint to the

punch, sort of like a bullwhip. It's important that you move only your rear foot, not your front foot, when you feint back. Otherwise, you'll probably find you've moved too far back, and your right cross won't be able to reach your opponent.

While the right cross is a powerful punch and deserves a lot of respect, you shouldn't be so intimidated by it that you think the only way to defend against it is by running from it or covering up. A right cross has strengths and weaknesses like any other technique, and there are several ways to counter it.

One way would be to bob to the left as your opponent throws his right. This puts you on the outside of your opponent and away from his punches. As soon as you bob, throw a left hook to his body. Land this punch once and he'll think twice about throwing his right hand again.

Another method of countering the right cross is to modify your left side body block slightly so you can cover your head with it. Take the punch on your arm and shoulder and roll back with it, allowing the force to dissipate. As soon as you've rolled,

allow the recoiling motion to bring you back to the front, and use the momentum to throw a counter right cross, straight back at your opponent.

This movement is especially useful if you're in a ring and you find yourself up against the ropes with someone pounding away at you, because you can roll back from the punch even further by leaning against the ropes.

A third option would involve first evading your opponent's punch by weaving under it. As you're going under his punch in

the first part of the weaving motion, punch to your opponent's body with a right hook.

Then, as you're coming back on the second part of the weaving motion, you're in a perfect position to throw a counter left hook to your opponent's jaw. Remember to pivot on your front foot as you hook.

COUNTERING THE LEFT HOOK

If your opponent is attacking with a left hook to your head, I recommend two basic counters. The first again uses the weave to evade the punch, and throwing a left hook to your opponent's body as you go under his punch.

You then come over the top of his left hook with a right hook to his jaw. This technique is basically the opposite of the last counter we did against the right cross.

If you're not able to weave to avoid an incoming left hook, either because your opponent's hook is too fast or your reactions are too slow, you may have to block his hook with your arm and glove. This is an acceptable defense, and you still have a counter available to you. I recommend simply throwing a left hook of your own immediately after

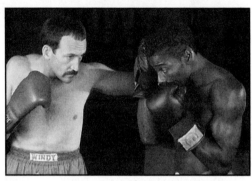

you block. Your hook may actually have a better chance of landing than his does, because he may drop his arm inadvertently after he hooks, leaving his head open to attack.

You may find yourself on the receiving end of a right hook, especially if you're working with a southpaw. The same counters, done in reverse, work in this situation as well. As the right hook is thrown, weave under it to

your left as you throw a right hook to your opponent's body. As you come out of the weave, counter with a left hook to his head. Or, if you block the hook instead of weaving out of the way, use your left arm and glove to bear the brunt of the punch, and counter with a right hook.

A kickboxer with good boxing skills will probably attack your body as much as possible, usually with hooks. You have several choices for counters in these situations, however, especially if your opponent is punching you offensively, as opposed to defensively.

The difference is the position of your arms: If your opponent is attacking you outright, as opposed to counterpunching off of your attack, your arms are likely to be at your sides in the on-guard position, instead of up and extended because you're punching. This makes it easier to block and counterpunch when your body is under attack.

If your opponent throws a left hook to your body, you have a couple of solid ways of dealing with it. One would be to body block with your right side, then counter with a left uppercut to his chin. This is a very simple, yet effective technique: One hand blocks, the other one punches. Also take note of the angles

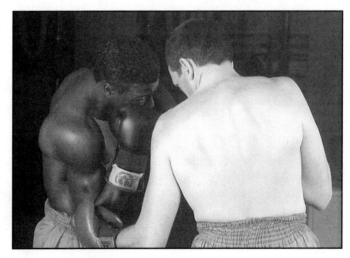

at work here. The hook is coming at
your side on a somewhat horizontal
plane, so you'll counter with a technique that travels vertically to the
target.

Another option for countering a left
hook to the body would be to again
body block with your right arm,
then immediately counter with a
right uppercut, continue with a left

hook to your opponent's chin, and finish him off with a right cross. Since
the uppercut comes from the same side that blocked the original attack, it
doesn't have quite the power that the left uppercut did in the previous
counter. Keep in mind, however, that the target is your opponent's chin, a
spot that doesn't have to be hit with a lot of force to be effective. The
uppercut also snaps your opponent's head up, which sets him up for the left
hook and the right cross.

COUNTERING THE RIGHT HOOK

If you're countering against a right
hook to the body, simply apply the
same counters in reverse. Body block
with your left arm, and counter with
a right uppercut to your opponent's

chin. (This is a very powerful
counter for the orthodox fighter. An
uppercut to the chin done by a
strong right arm could easily result
in a knockout.)

If you wish to counter with more than a single punch, body block left when your opponent throws the right hook,

uppercut to his chin with your left,

continue with a right cross and finish

with a left hook. This is a good counter against the southpaw, because it incorporates the standard right cross-left hook combination that's so effective against the left-handed fighter.

COUNTERING THE UPPERCUT

When defending against an uppercut, there are basically two things that will keep you from taking one of these punches on the chin, other than a feint or some movement.

The first one's simple: Distance. If you're working from either long-range or medium distance, you're not close enough to your opponent for him to use this punch. But if the battle's raging in close quarters, watch out for it.

Countering an uppercut to the chin requires that you first nullify the incoming punch. To do this, use the uppercut block mentioned earlier in the discussion on boxing defenses. You will probably use your rear hand for the block, but if the situation dictates otherwise, your lead hand

works as well. After stopping the punch, you're in a good position to throw either a left hook or a left uppercut of your own. Both are effective close-range punches, and if you counter your opponent's upper-cut successfully a couple of times, he's liable to stop throwing it.

When a fighter attacks you, he's usually got one thing on his mind—offense. By learning to counterpunch effectively, you can quickly turn your opponent's offense into your offense,

at a time when defense is the farthest thing from his mind and he's wide open to your shots.

KICKING COMBINATIONS

17

Imagine you could only use your legs...

I suppose it's no surprise a kickboxer nicknamed "Sugarfoot" likes to kick. Since my first interest in the martial arts as a kid, I've been fascinated by different kicking techniques and the people doing them.

But as much as I was influenced by the likes of Bruce Lee, Chuck Norris, Bill Wallace and Benny Urquidez, as I grew older my fascination grew not only from watching others, but from my own seemingly innate ability to mimic and perform the types of kicks these superstars were doing. This natural ability eventually led to competition, and my love of kicking led me to end a promising boxing career to pursue kickboxing full-time.

Now I'll detail some of my favorite kicking combinations which I've developed over the years. As usual, the focus will be on working these techniques independently, with the goal being to educate your legs to a high degree of kicking skill, flexibility and coordination.

To put yourself in the mindset I want you to have while you learn these techniques, imagine your hands are tied together in front of you and you have only your feet to defend yourself with. And as you practice these kicking combinations, look for places where you can alter them slightly to personalize them and make them more your own.

Not all of these techniques will work for you as they're shown here; some adjustments may be necessary to adapt them to your

fighting style or your physical makeup. Different body types have different strengths and weaknesses, and these are important factors you should give some thought to when assessing your kickboxing skills.

My body is well suited for speed and quickness; yours might be more power-oriented. This doesn't mean I can't generate any power with my kicks, or that you can't kick fast. It simply means, especially when you're first learning these kicks, some may be easier for you to master than others because of your musculature or genetic makeup.

And don't make any assumptions about the abilities of your opponent or training partner based solely on the way he or she is built. Invariably, you'll run across individuals at either end of the spectrum who possess abilities they don't look like they should. Joe Lewis is a good example.

Crowned full contact karate's first heavyweight world champion in 1974, Lewis possessed an incredible physique that was obviously powerful, but might cause some people to assume it would slow him down. Not hardly. Many of Lewis' opponents and sparring partners came away from an encounter with him in awe of not only his power, but his amazing speed. So much for assumptions.

Most kicking combos start with a kick thrown with your front leg, much like you use your jab to initiate many of the boxing sequences. Remember to keep your hands up to protect your head and face while kicking; don't let the fact you're not using your punches at the moment allow you to develop bad habits.

There will be some similarities in the kicking sequences to the boxing combinations, where you started with a jab and a right cross, then added a hook, and then an uppercut, and so forth. But mostly with kicking combos you'll change the levels you're attacking, with an overriding theme of getting your opponent used to certain kicks coming at him from certain directions, then switching your attack to a different target, or throwing a kick from your opposite side.

The importance of varying the levels you attack will now become even clearer, as the options afforded by kicking are greater than those by punching. Now you'll also have the lower body, specifically the thighs and calves, as targets.

LEFT FRONT KICK-RIGHT ROUND KICK

The first combination consists of a left front kick to the body, followed by a right round kick to the leg. Notice that the attack level sequence goes from middle to low; you now have the option of going after a low target due to the addition of the leg kick, and this should prove to be a major component of your fighting strategy.

A good kickboxer keeps his opponent guessing whether the next attack is going to be a punch or a kick, and where it's going to land. This combo is a real basic, effective one that should quickly become one of your "bread and butter" techniques. It can be followed with a variety of punches or, as we'll see in the next combo, another kick.

The front kick to the body usually gets the attention and respect of your opponent. It has a reasonably long reach and, since it comes straight at the body, is hard to avoid. Remember to extend your hips forward when executing the front kick, and then withdraw your kicking leg back to the chambered position before setting it down and throwing the round
kick. This makes it difficult for your opponent to parry and redirect your kick. Even if your opponent blocks the kick it's liable to knock him back. This gives you room to throw the kick to his thigh without crowding yourself. When you throw the leg kick, pivot fully on your post leg for maximum power.

This combination is also effective in a self-defense situation. Let's step out of the ring for a minute and imagine a scenario that goes something like this: You're walking up to your front door after a trip to the grocery store, and have bags in both arms. Before you can unlock your door and go inside, you're approached by someone who has chosen you as "victim *du jour*" and thinks you're an easy target because your hands are full.

You're forced to defend yourself, but there's no time to drop your packages and free your hands. This leaves your legs as your only resource to defend yourself with, but they should be sufficient. Fire that front kick at your assailant's midsection, then follow up with the round kick to the leg.

Since this could be a life-or-death situation, you may want to consider kicking your attacker in the knee with that round kick instead of the thigh. While I've seen men go down from one well-placed kick to the thigh, the same kick to the knee has the potential to inflict more damage and disable your assailant longer, giving you time to get away, call the authorities and go replace the eggs you dropped when you pivoted to throw your round kick.

This is a relatively safe combo to use in a self-defense situation, because both kicks are thrown to lower target areas, and you're facing your opponent the entire time. Avoid high or spinning kicks for self-defense, they are usually too risky, but a good rule of thumb is to attack with the first technique that pops into your mind, without hesitation.

FRONT KICK-RIGHT ROUND KICK-LEFT ROUND KICK

Like some of the boxing combinations we studied earlier, this next sequence starts off like the previous one, then adds another kick. I can't stress to you enough how important it is to mix up your combinations so you don't get stuck in any predictable patterns. As effective as they are, even the most unskilled opponent eventually catches on if you repeatedly throw the same combinations.

This combo starts with a front kick to the body and a right round kick to the leg, then adds a left round kick to your opponent's head. This one covers all the bases in terms of attack levels. You first attack the middle area, then the lower area and, just when your opponent thinks you're finished kicking and lets his guard down for a moment, you go upstairs with a head kick. Not only is it effective to go from a low kick to a high kick, this sequence also goes to the opposite side of your  opponent's body, in this case his head, which should add to his confusion.

From a technical standpoint, you'll need to practice making the transition from the round kick to the leg to the round kick to the head, because the distance involved might seem a little awkward at first.

If you find yourself too close to your training partner when you execute the round kick to his head, watch where you place your right foot after you withdraw your leg kick. The remedy may be a simple matter of setting that foot down a little further back than you normally would, which gives you a little more room between you and your partner.

When you practice these techniques, try to maintain a steady rhythm as you move from one kick to the next. And don't worry about performing these combos at warp speed right from the start; stick to a steady pace that allows you to concentrate on proper technique and execution. Speed is an asset only if it accompanies correct form. A garbage technique thrown fast is still garbage.

FRONT KICK-WHIPPING ROUND KICK

Our third kicking combination is a front kick to the body followed by a whipping round kick to the head, which is probably the best example of the kicking equivalent to "the old one-two." Notice the progression of the combos that start with a front kick: You first went to your opponent's thigh with your leg kick, then in the second combo you repeated that movement and added a left round kick to his head. Now you throw your front kick to his body, then go immediately to his head with a right whipping round kick.

This is a simple combination, yet it takes on a very bold character, especially if you have used the two previous combos to set up this one. One minute you and your opponent are moving back and forth, trading shots, and in the space of a heartbeat you launch one of your most powerful kicks, a rear leg whipping round kick, directly at his head. No matter how experienced your opponent is, no matter how many times someone has tried to kick him in the head, I guarantee if you throw this combo correctly, with proper speed, power and intent, he'll have no choice but to take you and your abilities seriously.

Even if your opponent manages to block or avoid the whipping round kick, you can easily change the tone of the entire exchange with this one combination. This combo means business. But use it sparingly. This is a "big gun" technique, and it's often advisable to save the big guns for special occasions. Showing your opponent this combo too many times probably lessens its effectiveness. Use some of the other combos to create an opening for this one, then go for it.

And here's a tip out of the official sneaky handbook: Throw a few of the front kick-round kick to the leg combos at your opponent, and throw the leg kicks hard. Then throw another front kick in preparation for the whipping round kick, and just before you throw the round kick, glance down at your opponent's leg. If you're lucky, your opponent will think you're telegraphing another leg kick and he'll shift his focus to that area just as you launch a kick at his head. This should improve your chances of landing the technique.

FRONT KICK-SPINNING BACK KICK

The front kick to the body followed by a spinning back to the body is the last combination that uses a lead leg front kick to initiate the attack, and it

completes our strategy of trying to keep your opponent guessing where the second kick is going to land.

The earlier combinations used a kick to the body before kicking to his leg or either side of his head. This combo is useful if your opponent has figured out your strategy and is expecting you to kick one of these areas after you kick to his body. If this proves to be the case, a front kick followed by a spinning back kick, both to the body, may catch your opponent unaware, as he may be raising his guard in anticipation of a kick to his head, or looking to check your leg kick.

Don't rush the front kick; fire a solid one to his midsection, pivot, and look over your shoulder at your opponent before you throw the back kick to check your opponent's reaction. This is another big gun technique, and should also be used sparingly to maximize its

effectiveness. This combo is a great equalizer, and I find it useful when I'm training or sparring with someone who is much bigger than I am. Often a larger person tries to crowd you and intimidate you with his size, and a spinning back kick is a great way to balance the scales.

And a front kick doesn't have to be aimed at your opponent's midsection any more than a jab has to be thrown at your opponent's face. I instruct my students and fighters to stick an occasional jab in their opponent's belly. It's a bit unorthodox, but it effectively sets up other punches, especially the overhand right.

It's perfectly acceptable to aim your front kick at face level, and you may find it beneficial to do so occasionally. The height and angle tend to make it more difficult to thrust the kick, so you pretty much have to snap it out, but thrusting a front kick when the target is someone's face really isn't necessary anyway. Just be sure you bring your knee up to a good chambered position, form the proper weapon with your foot and snap the kick out and back quickly. Even if the kick doesn't land, it tends to cause your opponent to lean back to get his face away from the kick, and this creates openings for other punches and kicks.

This combo could also be used to attack your opponent high, as you could throw the front kick to your opponent's face, and follow it with a spinning side kick to the same spot.

Left Side Kick-Spinning Back Kick

Another combo that uses a lead leg kick to set up the spinning back kick is the side kick-spinning back kick. A good nickname for this combo would be "Double Trouble," as each kick by itself can cause a lot of trouble for your opponent, while the two paired in a combination...well, you get the idea.

This pairing creates a combination that spells only one thing: Power. The side kick is probably the most powerful kick you can throw with your front

leg, and the spinning back kick is the most powerful kick, period. Either of these kicks thrown to the midsection will knock your opponent back several feet if he blocks them, or drop him if he doesn't.

With the side kick you can go either to the body or the head. As I've mentioned, it's rare to see the side kick used in the kickboxing world, and even rarer to see it used to the head. Consequently, you'll have a very formidable weapon in your arsenal if you master the side kick, especially if you can throw it high, and in conjunction with other kicks.

When performing the side kick with the spinning back kick you'll need to make a slight adjustment in your footwork. After you've side kicked, instead of placing your kicking foot back where it was, set it down slightly to the right. This initiates the turning motion necessary to spin and kick, and aligns your body and kicking leg with your target. At this point, it's a simple matter of pivoting to complete the spin and executing the back kick. Remember to tuck your chin into your shoulder for protection, and keep your eyes on your opponent as you spin.

A combination I don't think is seen in kickboxing as much as it should be is the double switch step-round kick. This is odd, because throwing this technique in multiples is a staple of the Muay Thai kicking diet. Granted, this is a tough combo to learn and it requires a substantial amount of energy to execute. I suppose that's why it's not seen very often.

Although you may find this movement a difficult one to master, once you've got it down you'll have a weapon that combines power and speed in rapid-fire succession. Each kick derives its speed and power from the one before it, and you may find yourself throwing them not only in sets of two, but also in threes and fours. The Thai use this combination like a battering ram, usually to the body of their opponents. Even if an opponent protects his rib cage with his arms, the damage adds up over the course of a match.

When performing this combination you can go to your opponent's body with the first kick and then go to his head with the second, or attack his body with both kicks. Either one is effective. Using the body / head option brings attention to one area to create an opening in another. Doubling up to the body increases the chances of slipping one of the kicks under your opponent's guard and connecting to his vulnerable rib cage.

As I said, this is a physically demanding combo, so you'll want to drill this one a lot in practice before attempting it while sparring. Use your shin as the striking surface on the kick to the body, and as

your kicking leg comes behind you after the first kick, don't let that foot plant all the way down. Instead, stay on the ball of your foot to control the descent of your leg, then use your calf muscles to spring off for the next kick.

As a preventive measure, leg check with the leg that's not kicking anytime you spin back into position after missing the high kick. In this case, as you spin back into position after the kick to the head, check with your right leg. This is a good practice to get into, as a smart fighter often counters with a kick to your post leg if he evades the high kick. If your opponent sees you're prepared for this counter, he'll have to rethink his strategy.

REAR LEG FRONT KICK-LEFT ROUND KICK

A rear leg front kick to the body coupled with a left round kick to the head is another very basic, yet very effective technique, and it's sort of the reverse of the front kick combos we started off with. While I don't often initiate combinations with my rear leg, this one fits into the big gun category, and it's nice to pull it out of the holster every once in a while. It also has the advantage of bringing me back to my original orthodox stance if I choose, depending on how I throw the second kick.

When you execute the front kick with your rear leg, thrust your hips forward to drive the ball of your foot into your opponent and through his guard. The front kick delivered from the rear has a lot of power, and will likely force your opponent backward. This gives you room to throw your round kick, which comes from what is now your back leg, because you planted what was your back leg forward after you front kicked. As always, re-chamber your kicking leg before setting it down.

Use the momentum forward to help you throw your round kick to your opponent's head; you can snap the round kick and set down in your original stance, or whip it, pivot on your right foot and spin back to the southpaw stance. If you choose the latter, this is another place where it's advisable to leg check with your right leg, just in case your opponent tries to counter you with a leg kick.

REAR ROUND KICK-SPINNING BACK KICK

The next combination reverses the pattern of attacking your opponent's body to open up his head by utilizing a round kick to the head and a spinning back kick to the body. Like the previous combo, it initiates the sequence with the rear leg, instead of the lead leg. Since the first kick is coming off your rear leg, there's a chance your opponent will see it in time to block it.

This doesn't mean it's not a valid technique; throw it with the intention of knocking out your opponent, which is what it's liable to do if it gets through. An experienced fighter may get his guard up in time, which is just what you want.

As soon as your first kick lands, drop your leg, pivot, look over your shoulder and fire the spinning back kick. To return to your original stance, plant your kicking foot, step out to the left with your right foot and pivot back into place. Your opponent may not block, but rather feint back from your first kick.

If this happens, it's often a sign that he's going to rush you with a counter. Let him. With him bridging the gap between you and your spinning back kick speeding toward him, he's in for a head-on collision, and he'll get the worst of it.

Hook Kick-Snapping Round Kick

Let's switch gears somewhat, and look at a technique that's a bit more advanced. I advocate educating your lead leg as much as possible, and recommend investing the time and energy necessary to become proficient with a hook kick-snapping round kick combination.

This is another combo you won't see a lot in kickboxing, which highlights the advantage of being able to do it. I find this comes in handy if I need to break up the tempo of a match, since the reaction of my opponent after I throw it is usually something like: "What was that, and where did it come from?"

You may find this a difficult technique to master because you're kicking with the same leg and both kicks are at head level, so you may want to start out by practicing the kicks at a lower height. This allows you to gradually develop the balance necessary, while enabling you to clearly see how well you're performing the various components of the kicks.

Several types of striking pads are available that you could use to practice these kicks, or you could simply have your coach or training partner hold a folded paper sack or the lid of a shoebox as a target. Focus on proper form first, then work on the speed of the kicks as your ability to kick higher progresses. Once you're able to throw both kicks at head level, you can begin to fine-tune the movement.

When I throw this combo, the hook kick is used more as a distraction and a set-up than anything else. Still, you must throw it realistically and correctly, as a good opponent will sense you're up to something if you don't. Besides, if you can hit him with the hook kick, there's no reason not to.

Raise your knee to achieve the height necessary to kick to your opponent's head, and extend your hook kick out at his head. The beauty of following your hook kick with a round kick is twofold. If you hit your opponent with your hook kick, your foot and leg will probably still follow through to the chamber position for the round kick, which allows you to kick him again on the other side of his head, just to make sure he got your point.

If your hook kick misses or he evades it, you get a second chance to catch him with your round kick. A round kick coming off of a hook kick is extremely fast; something in the physiology of the movement seems to add speed to the second kick.

As your hook kick follows through, be sure to change the position of your kicking foot, pointing your toes down so your instep is now your striking surface. If you're having a hard time maintaining your balance, check that your weight is centered over your post leg.

The common error to guard against with this combination is the tendency for the kicking leg and the chambered knee position to drop between the two kicks, which steals the necessary height from the snapping round kick. Two factors prevent this from happening: Your weight being properly centered over your post leg, and having sufficient strength in the muscle groups that hold your leg up. Nail these factors, and you'll nail the combo.

These combinations should give you a pretty solid foundation in regard to basic kicking strategy and tactics. As with the boxing combos, spend the time necessary to become as adept with your kicks as you are your hands. I also encourage you to experiment with different combinations and sequences, and find what works best for you.

Don't disregard something as useless just because it didn't work the first time you tried it; diligent practice and patience allow you to see if certain techniques work for you or not. Take the time to do it right.

KICKING COUNTERS

There's a strategy in many martial arts styles that says: Fight your opponent opposite of the way he fights you. If he attacks you in a linear style, counter him with a circular one. If he uses power techniques, retaliate with speed techniques. If he punches you, kick him. If he kicks you, punch him. Boxing has its own version of this strategy, which my old coach Ed Couzens used to tell me: "Box a slugger and slug a boxer."

This is a sound principle of fighting and one I've used often, but I find on occasion it's better to fight fire with fire, and show my opponent I'm better at whatever he's doing than he is. When two fighters of similar ability and skill level are sparring or competing against each other, the outcome's often decided by which person has the superior mental game plan. Part of this game plan should be to show your opponent that you're skilled in all aspects of fighting, and no matter what he does, you can do it better.

Sometimes fighters who do any type of kicking, whether it's a kickboxer, a karate fighter or whatever, have a tendency to give up on their kicking ability if they run across someone they think is a better kicker than they are. This can be intimidating, and a little humbling, but it's also an unproductive mindset that feeds on itself.

Let's say Joe and Tommy are working out one night in the gym. Joe considers himself a pretty good kicker, but Tommy's having a great night kicking, and is pretty much nailing Joe at will. Instead of rising to the occasion and increasing the number or type or speed or strength of his kicks, or countering the kicks from Tommy, Joe all but gives up on his kicking, and tries to make do with just his punching techniques.

Having abandoned the kicking half of his arsenal, Joe becomes little more than a moving heavy bag for Tommy. And Tommy, motivated by how well his kicks are working, especially now that Joe isn't kicking much or countering, starts to throw more kicks, faster kicks, stronger kicks and different kicks. Tommy's having a blast. This, of course, only makes things worse for Joe, and the cycle continues.

Don't allow yourself to be intimidated by a good kicker. Instead, show him you're no slouch in that department yourself. Just because someone's trying to kick you doesn't mean you have to stand there and take it. Here are some counter movements for some of the more common kicks you're liable to have thrown at you. Good counters keep your opponent from dominating you with their kicks, and they tend to reduce the number of shots you take, which reduces your chance of injury.

COUNTERING FRONT KICKS

Redirecting is probably the best way to set up your counter against a front kick, regardless of whether the kick comes from your opponent's front or rear leg. Proper redirecting puts your opponent at a disadvantage in terms of stance and positioning, which creates openings for you to counter.

Trying to block a front kick generally entails dropping your forearms somewhat and covering your midsection, leaving your head dangerously open to attack. If nothing else, your arms take a beating, and there's always the chance that a front kick could glance off of your arms and hit you in the solar plexus or ribs anyway. A properly executed redirection avoids this problem, because it moves your body out of danger. I'll take the "not get hit" option every chance I get.

If your opponent front kicks with his lead leg, redirect it to your left, and

counter with a round kick with your rear leg, usually to your opponent's kicking leg, as it will probably be the closest leg to you. However, if your redirecting motion spins your opponent further than you expected, his rear leg is probably the one to kick. In other words, kick the leg that's closest to you. Make sure your hands are up for protection, as your counter leg kick puts you in close with your opponent. When practicing this counter with a partner, experiment by adding some punches to your counter as well, so you get the feel of using your kicks and punches together.

If your opponent front kicks with his rear leg, take a slight step to your left

and redirect to your right. Then pivot and counter with a round kick, using your lead leg to attack whichever leg is closest to you, which is probably his kicking leg. Since your kick is coming off your front leg, be sure you pivot fully to attain maximum power behind your kick.

Another option would be to strike lower on his leg, just below his calf muscle and turn your leg kick into a sweep. Be careful when practicing this movement, however. If you actually sweep your partner, make sure you do it on a mat that offers some padding, or in a boxing ring with a mat that isn't too hard. And always get your training partner's consent before you sweep him, as falling is an art in itself, and he may not know how to do it properly. Because if you sweep him, he's going down.

This counter reflects another strategy in the fighting arts: Attack whatever you were attacked with. In other words, hit the part of your opponent's body that he used to hit you. If he used his right leg to kick you, kick his right leg. If he's jabbing you incessantly, punch and kick his left arm to the point where he won't be able to use it to jab with. It may sound vicious, but this is fighting, and it works.

COUNTERING SIDE KICKS

Though it's a strong technique, a side kick can also be redirected. It's a little trickier than redirecting a front kick, but it can be done. Keep in mind that a side kick is usually more powerful than a front kick, so the consequences of messing up the counter are costlier. Pay close attention.

As the kick comes toward you, redirect it to the left as you would a front kick (*photo 1*), then counter with a round kick to your opponent's post leg (*photo 2*). If you like, you can step out to the right slightly and really blast your leg kick, kind of like kicking a soccer ball. Done correctly, this is really painful for your opponent, because his post leg position for the side kick exposes the back of his thigh, a more tender area than the front, to your leg kick counter.

Another way to counter a side kick is

to again redirect the kick, but this time step back with your left leg as you redirect, allowing your opponent's kick to follow through. The step back puts you in a right side forward stance; keep your right arm up for protection or extend it to push your opponent back and create room to throw a rear leg round kick. Depending on the amount of space available, you can throw the kick to his leg, his body, or use a whipping round kick to his head.

COUNTERING SPINNING KICKS

Perhaps the most intimidating and difficult kicks to defend against or counter are the spinning back kick and its cousin, the spinning side kick. Both are extremely fast and powerful, and it's tempting either to cover up, take the kick on your forearms and hope for the best, or run away from it. While it's advisable to have a healthy respect for this kick, you don't have to be afraid of it, because there are several ways to effectively counter it.

For the first counter, as your opponent spins and starts to extend his back kick, step out to your left, just as you would if you were redirecting a rear leg front kick, to get your body out of the line of fire. You're relatively safe in this position; it's similar to being in the eye of a hurricane.

This position is also advantageous because it puts you in your opponent's blind spot. As soon as you step, pivot and kick the outside of your opponent's post leg with a lead leg round kick, striking with your shin.

A slight variation of this counter would be to again step to your left as your opponent attempts his kick, only this time kick as you step, using your rear leg to shoot a round kick to the inside of your opponent's post leg. This version is probably the simplest and quickest method, and relatively easy to learn. Again, use your shin as the striking surface.

COUNTERING HOOK KICKS

It may be rare for someone to throw a hook kick at you, but since I've shown you how to throw it, I should show you how to defend against it. To counter a hook kick to my head, I use a reinforced block to stop the kick outright. I could weave under the hook kick, but if my opponent has an educated leg he could follow up with a round kick before he sets his foot down, and tag me as my head comes back up from the weave.

Blocking the kick doesn't leave my opponent as many options to follow up with, because the block tends to cause his leg to drop back to the floor. A hook kick travels such a short distance, it doesn't have time to pick up the speed and momentum of other kicks, so you should be successful in blocking it. As soon as you

block, counter with a rear leg round kick to the outside of your opponent's post leg, striking with your shin.

Another method of countering the hook kick is to again use the reinforced

block, then step out to the right and throw a lead leg round kick to the inside of your opponent's post leg. Because of the close range, kick with your shin rather than with your instep. Like the spinning back kick counters, this second one is the simplest and quickest version.

It's imperative you practice these counters with quickness in mind. There is no time for you to hesitate between your blocks and your counters; you must follow up immediately or your opponent will retreat out of range or, worse, counter your counter and smack you good. A hook kick is also a good place to turn your counter kick into a sweep, as the position of the kick puts your opponent virtually on top of you.

COUNTERING SNAPPING ROUND KICKS

To effectively counter a snapping round kick you must first eliminate your opponent's ability to throw the kick in multiples of two or more. Simply blocking the kick is not enough; if you block the first one and go for your counter you're liable to eat a second one. Even if you don't get kicked, you won't have as good an opportunity to counter, because you've done nothing

to stop his ability to keep throwing kicks at your head. (Keep in mind the similarities between a snapping round kick and a jab: Both are effective at keeping an opponent off of you, and they work just as well when you're on the receiving end of them.)

To put yourself in a better position to counter a snapping round kick,

you'll need to redirect your opponent's kick down as well as block it, to eliminate the possibility of multiple kicks. Against a kick coming to your right side, block the kick with a reinforced block, then open your left glove and wrap it around the

ankle of your opponent's kicking leg. Push his leg down and across in front of you, and immediately counter with a rear leg round kick to your opponent's kicking leg.

If the snapping round kick is coming to your left side, simply reverse the movements: Block with both forearms, wrap your opponent's kicking leg with your

right glove, parry it down and across in front of you, then counter with a lead leg round kick to his kicking leg.

You may think you'll never be able to do this, but it's not as difficult as you might think. This is where your time in the gym with a good coach and training partner comes into play. Practice this counter using the give-and-take method: One person kicks at a slow to medium pace while the other blocks, parries and counters. Then switch roles, giving each other feedback as to how everything feels. Gradually increase the speed, and eventually you'll be ready to try this counter while sparring.

While simply evading a power kick like a switch step or a whipping round kick affords less wear and tear on your body than blocking does, there are some legitimate ways of blocking and countering these kicks. Granted, your forearms may take a beating from these methods, so you may want to use some discretion as to how often you use them. But I'd rather take these kicks on my arms than my rib cage, and occasionally you'll run into situations where blocking is the only option you have, so it's wise to have a couple of blocking methods on file should the need arise.

Both of these techniques are unique in that they include punches to set up the kicking counters. While you haven't put your punches and kicks together yet, the kicks you're defending against require an aggressive response, so you'll use two power punches to set up the counter kicks.

When a power round kick comes to your right side, stop it with your reinforced block, then immediately throw a right cross-left hook combination to your opponent's head. Don't get in a hurry to throw the

punches. You must block that kick before you can do anything else—missing the block could result in some broken ribs, which will let all of the air out of both you and your counter.

The punches also position your body for your counterkick, a rear leg round kick to his thigh. (Once again, which leg you kick depends on your opponent's stance; it's usually best to kick the one closest to you.) As I've said, there's no room for hesitation anywhere in these counters. As soon as you block, you punch, and as soon as you punch, you kick. The punches not only get your opponent off of you and set up your counter, they add power to the kick if the momentum flows properly.

If a power round kick comes to your left side, stop it with the reinforced block, then throw a left hook to your opponent's jaw, followed by a right cross. This puts you in position to throw your counter kick, a lead leg round kick to his thigh. You could also throw the left hook-right cross and counter with a switch step round kick to your opponent's thigh, which you may do instinctively once you become comfortable with the switch step movement.

Kicking counters are a weak spot in the armor of many martial artists and kickboxers. I'm not sure why that is. Many fighters seem content trading shots with their opponents, as if they're taking turns kicking each other. Personally, I find this boring as a competitor, as well as a stupid way to treat your body, and I'm sure it's less than exciting for the spectators in the audience.

From a self-defense standpoint, it's just plain dangerous. If you're forced to defend yourself, you want to dish out as much punishment as you can while taking as little as possible. The way you train is the way you react; getting in the habit of countering kicks instead of just taking them certainly works in your favor, whether you're in the ring or on the street.

KNEE AND ELBOW COMBOS

Devastatingly effective in self-defense

The last of the combinations we'll focus on are using your knees and elbows in close-quarters fighting. When working with knees and elbows, never forget these are strong, brutal techniques, and you must use caution whenever practicing them with a partner.

It takes very little for an elbow strike to split open an eyebrow or break a nose, so you should either practice these techniques at half speed, or put on your protective gear while you train.

But the same aspect of these techniques that necessitates caution is what makes them so effective. It's probably safe to assume that whatever you hit with a knee or an elbow will hurt worse than you will.

THE LEFT ELBOW-RIGHT KNEE

The first combo pairs a left elbow to the face with a right knee to the stomach. Your left elbow comes down across your opponent's face in a cutting motion, and your goal is to bash whatever you hit, whether it's him or his guard.

This may knock his

guard down, which would open him up for other strikes. If it does, great! Hit him with something else. If it doesn't, he's going to have sore arms, so you're still making progress. You then immediately grab his head and pull him toward you as you thrust your hips forward, driving a

straight knee into his midsection.

THE RIGHT ELBOW-SWITCH STEP, FRONT KNEE

Reversing what you just did, you'll throw an elbow from your rear side, followed by a switch step-front knee to your opponent's stomach. A rear elbow is especially strong, because to make contact with your elbow requires that you follow through and torque even more than you do with a right cross.

After securing your headlock, switch step and drive your front knee forward. You'll know that you're becoming adept with this motion when you're able to quickly secure a strong hold on your opponent's neck and, almost simultaneously, throw your hips back and switch step, pulling him toward you as you knee him.

Next we'll use two elbows to set up the knee strike. You'll throw your lead elbow first, followed by your rear elbow, before grabbing your opponent and executing a rear knee.

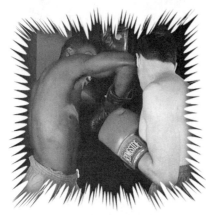

The power generated by the torso position for both of these elbow strikes is quite impressive: Either one is easily capable of knocking someone out. When you secure the headlock, experiment with taking a short step backward as you prepare to knee. This pulls your opponent off-balance and helps you generate momentum for your knee strike.

Two elbow strikes can also be used to set up a knee from the side. First throw the front elbow, then the rear elbow, as you did in the previous combination. After securing the headlock, replace your left foot with your right by doing a short hop to your left.

As your leg leaves the floor, raise your left knee out to the side at a 90-degree angle, and bring your knee into your opponent's side as you pull him toward your knee. This version comes in handy if you're having trouble penetrating your opponent's defenses with a straight knee, because it probably won't be expected from the side.

You could also use this in a combination with a straight knee, using the same knee to execute both versions, or alternating knees, using your lead leg for the side knee, and your rear leg for the straight knee.

You can also use either a front or a rear elbow to set up a knee to the front of your opponent's thigh. This is an effective weapon to use in a clinch, and it has the effect of wearing down your opponent. This would be another situation where you could combine a side knee with this technique for added results.

THE VERTICAL ELBOW-STRAIGHT KNEE

Probably the simplest elbow to throw is the vertical elbow. It's also a great way to open an opponent up for a straight knee to his body. Using your lead arm, raise your elbow up so it connects under the point of your opponent's chin, not with his throat.

This should force his head to pop up, which in turn opens his upper body and torso up. This is your invitation to launch a hard, straight knee into his body. Don't grab your opponent's head on this one, as that would defeat the purpose of popping his head up.

You can also switch the order, and start with a rear elbow to your opponent's chin, followed by a switch step straight knee to his body. Remember to keep your hands up to protect yourself. This is especially important when you're close enough to elbow your opponent. Don't forget, he's close enough to hit you back!

While these knee and elbow combos are effective in the ring, they're devastating on the street in self-defense. Many attackers expect your first move to be a knee, probably to the groin, and not only does your elbow to the face surprise him, it makes him forget he was expecting the knee, opening him up for the finish.

Executing any of these techniques successfully will almost certainly leave your attacker balled up on the ground, gasping for air. This is your time to run. I've talked about self-defense a number of times, and I can't stress its purpose enough: To get away unharmed.

Don't stand there and wait for him to get up, thinking you can practice another one of your combos on him. Real life is not like the movies. You may just find out he's armed. You're likely to find he's mad, and you've definitely lost the advantage of surprise. Run. When you get the chance, get out of there.

When practicing these basic movements, keep in mind that you are not limited to only using these techniques with each other. Look for places to weave the other techniques you've learned together with these knee and elbow strikes.

For example, you could practice a combination where you threw a jab, followed by a leg kick from your rear leg, landed in a southpaw stance, threw an overhand left elbow, grabbed your opponent and finished him off with a left knee to the body. Okay, maybe I got a little carried away.

But another, easier possibility would be to throw a lead leg front kick, followed by an overhand rear elbow and a rear knee. With enough time spent on these techniques individually, eventually you'll amaze yourself with how creative you've become, and how many new combinations you're coming up with.

HAND AND 2 FEET COMBOS

Time for a little fun

Now that you've learned your boxing and kicking combinations, it's time to get down to the heart of the matter: Putting your hands and feet together to become the best kickboxer you can be. Ultimately, you'll want to be able to set up a kick with a punch and a punch with a kick. The following combinations aren't the only ones that I use, but they represent a good cross section of my arsenal.

These techniques adhere strongly to the basics and are strategically sound. Study them, dissect them, extract whatever you can from them, and then throw out everything that doesn't work for you. Only after giving this material a thorough examination in your mind and in the gym will you be able to decide how much of it you can add to your repertoire.

When combining kicks and punches, distancing (the study and application of the most advantageous distance between you and your opponent) becomes a major factor. It's painfully obvious that it's difficult to punch someone who has his foot in your face or guts. Conversely, when someone's standing nose to nose with you, both of his fists raining down punches, you might find it hard to execute your favorite kick.

Distancing isn't difficult to learn, given the above incentives, but it will take some study on your part to learn to judge the gap between you and your opponent and know which technique is best suited to bridge that gap.

The on-guard position of your hands becomes very important, too. Some kickers are notorious for not keeping their hands up, especially when they're throwing a kick. Try this with an opponent who has good boxing skills and he'll think Christmas came early. Good punches and hand speed have often been an ace up my sleeve, especially in my matches with Thai fighters.

After my first match with Muay Thai champion Sakad Petchyindee, reporters questioned him about his apparent hesitation during our bout. He attributed this caution to my boxing skills, something he wasn't used to. Thai fighters tend to emphasize kicking over boxing techniques, although they've made great strides in the last few years. Sakad respected my punches enough to alter his normal game plan.

On the flip side, I've had fights where I relied heavily on kicks to deal with a good puncher. Way back in the amateur days of my career, I fought a very hard puncher from Seattle named Torres who came to kickboxing from amateur boxing. He was a Golden Gloves champ, and I knew he was going to be a handful in the punching department. Rather than try to slug it out with him, I relied on my kicking skills to dictate the course of the fight.

My boxing was good enough to discourage him whenever we got into close quarters, and I landed enough leg kicks that the match was stopped in the third round. The kicks had taken their toll, and he couldn't walk anymore. The better rounded your fighting skills are, the more strategy you're able to employ.

FRONT KICK-JAB-RIGHT CROSS

The front kick-jab-right cross combo is a good example of using a kick to bridge the gap between you and your opponent, putting you close enough to punch. A front kick is one of the safest kicks you can throw. It can be thrown quickly from your fighting stance, and it doesn't require as much balance as some of the other kicks. Also, when throwing it you enjoy the

advantage of facing your opponent, which makes it easy to throw straight punches, such as the jab and the right, before or after.

I like to use the front kick to my opponent's body to shake him up and move his concentration away from his head. Then, instead of pulling the kick back and planting my foot in its original position, I plant it slightly in front of me as I simultaneously shoot the jab. As soon as the jab is coming back to its on-guard position, I fire my right hand. This is another fundamental combo that should see a lot of use in your routine. There's nothing fancy about it, just good solid basics that combine economy of movement with very little risk.

FRONT KICK-JAB-RIGHT CROSS-LEFT HOOK-REAR ROUND KICK

The combination of a front kick-jab-right cross-left hook-rear round kick to the leg starts out the same as the previous technique, then adds a couple of moves at the end. After throwing the kick, jab and right cross, you're in an ideal position to throw a left hook and follow it up with a rear round kick to your opponent's leg. The left hook is a natural follow-up to the right cross, and the pivot that goes with it

positions your body to apply maximum torque to your leg kick.

It may appear the left hook puts you too close to your opponent to use a leg kick, but that's not the case. The left hook can be thrown close or wide, depending on the circumstances. If you throw it wide, then obviously there's ample room for the leg kick.

If you throw the hook close, the round kick to the leg kick can be adjusted slightly and still be thrown effectively. To do this, bend your kicking leg back to about a half-folded position, and exaggerate the pivot of your post foot. This will allow the proper area of your shin to make contact with your opponent's thigh with sufficient force. Put some time in on the heavy bag practicing this version of the leg kick. It comes in handy in close quarters combat and few fighters expect a leg kick when you're this close.

JAB-REAR ROUND KICK-FRONT ROUND KICK

Next is a jab-rear round kick-front round kick. In this combination you use a jab to set up two kicks, one to either side of your opponent's body. I like this one because not only does my opponent have to deal with my jab in his face, he then has to contend with one round kick to his leg, and another to his head from the opposite side.

Since the attack sequence goes from high to low to high, and from front to right to left, there's a good chance you'll catch him off guard and at least one of these shots will penetrate his defenses. You may rush the jab and throw it incorrectly because you're focusing on the kicks you're about to throw. This is a common mistake, and a dangerous one. This is also an example of how important your coach or training partner is, because this is the type of error you may not realize

you're doing, but a good trainer or workout partner will notice and point it out to you.

You must be sure any punch you throw, whether to initiate a combination or to set up other techniques, is thrown correctly and with realistic intent. Your preference in this case should be to connect with the jab, then proceed to kick your opponent in the leg and the head. If your jab misses for any reason, you have the two kicks to follow up with, but don't throw the jab thinking it's going to miss, or it's merely a prelude to your kicks. A good opponent won't take your attacks seriously if you don't throw them seriously.

DOUBLE JAB-RIGHT ROUND KICK

A double jab-right round kick with the shin to the body can be an extremely intimidating combination that has about the same result as a speeding locomotive—it runs right over your opponent. Even if he blocks your kick, it will still be painful enough to have been effective, as a

round kick quickly takes its toll on a person's forearms. When using this combo, fire your jabs hard and fast, and let them pull your body forward.

This creates the momentum for the kick, and drives your opponent back.

The jabs should also cause him to raise his arms, exposing his side and rib cage to your kick. Leave your arm extended in front of his face after the second jab as you stutter step and fire your rear leg round kick. This extended arm serves two purposes: It distracts your opponent, and it keeps your head and face protected. Practice the components of this combination at a slow-to-moderate pace until you can execute it in an explosive manner. If it's not explosive, keep practicing.

RIGHT CROSS-SWITCH STEP ROUND KICK

A right cross-switch step round kick with the shin combines two power techniques in a deceptive manner. Normally, punches and kicks from your lead side initiate a combination, followed by punches and kicks from your rear side. This follows the accepted school of thought that you should start with speed and finish with power, which, generally, is sound advice.

Occasionally, however, it's advantageous to change this order, as a smart opponent will quickly figure out your strategy if you fall into a predictable pattern of attack. This combo is a good way to break that pattern, because your initial movement comes from the rear, from your right hand throwing the right cross,

followed by a kick from your lead leg, rather than your rear leg. A lead right cross is a strong way to get your opponent's attention, and should distract him enough to open up his midsection to your switch step round kick. In such close quarters, you'll be using your shin as the striking surface. As with the previous technique, leave your punching arm extended and in your opponent's face while you switch step and kick.

JAB-SIDE KICK-SPINNING BACK KICK

Going back to using the lead hand to set up your opponent, this sequence consists of a jab-side kick-spinning back kick. In this combination, after the jab both kicks are thrown in a straight line at your opponent's midsection. This could be useful for a couple of reasons.

If you've been using your jab to set up kicks or punches that go to the side of your opponent's body, he may be open to attack up the middle. And if he's

not, straight kicks are often more difficult to block or evade than ones coming at angles. The kicks used here are not only thrown in a straight line, they're two of the strongest kicks you have. You stand a good chance of penetrating your opponent's defenses with them, and even if they don't they'll certainly gain his respect.

This is a good combo to use against a bigger or stronger opponent, either offensively or defensively, as you could use it to back him up or keep him off of you. As with previous examples, leave your jab extended as you chamber and fire your side kick. Be sure to bring your leg back to chamber before setting it down, as opposed to just letting it fall down after you kick. This puts your foot in a proper position to pivot for the spinning back kick. Just letting your leg drop probably puts you too close to your opponent to spin.

Your stance for the second kick depends on the effect of your first kick. If your side kick knocks your opponent backward, you'll probably have to plant your pivot foot slightly more forward than usual, so the spinning back kick will reach him. As with any spinning technique, be sure to look over your shoulder before you fire the kick.

The next combination, a feint-jab-lead snapping round kick to the head-right cross to the body-left hook to the jaw, attacks your opponent from just about every angle possible. A feint with the head or shoulder helps you connect with your jab, and it's a good way to "test the waters" of your opponent's defenses.

Some fighters are hard to hit with a jab; they bob or feint back well, or they may simply be extremely wary, a bit jumpy, or just plain fast. If I run into one of these guys, I like to feint to see what their reaction is, and base my strategy accordingly. If your opponent doesn't react, you can probably hit him with a single jab. If he does, you may have to double jab, or throw two single jabs with a slight pause between them, to hopefully catch him with the second one. Or, as in this case, you feint and jab as a prelude to the snapping round kick to your opponent's face. The round kick puts you within range to dig a right cross into your opponent's body, which is immediately followed by a left hook to his jaw.

An important point to remember here is you're throwing two punches at close range at your opponent, who also knows how to punch and kick. In other words, *keep your hands up*. It's common to drop the position of the hand that isn't punching; this is careless and dangerous, especially in close quarters.

Jab-Right Cross-Left Hook-Rear Round Kick

Look at the attack levels of a jab-right cross-left hook to the body-rear round kick to the leg, and you'll see you're working your way down your opponent's body with progressively harder hitting shots. Your jab, a speed technique, initiates the combination,

and is followed by a right cross to your opponent's chin. As you withdraw your right cross, you drill a left hook to the right side of his body, and finish with a rear leg round kick to his left leg.

You've not only worked your way down his body, you've attacked his middle and both sides as well. This pattern should keep your opponent too busy blocking or evading to counter, creating openings for your attacks. There's a tendency to drop your right hand when hooking to the body, so concentrate on keeping your guard up, as you'll be within range of your opponent's left hook.

JAB-RIGHT CROSS-DOUBLE SWITCH STEP ROUND KICK

This next combination starts with a jab-right cross, then adds a double switch step round kick to the body and head of your opponent. Granted, doubling up a switch step kick will take some practice before you get the hang of it. It's a tough kick to master. It takes balance and timing and you have to fight gravity with the second kick, because you're going from the middle level to the upper level.

Once you've acquired the agility to perform this kick, however, you'll probably be the only kid on your block with this toy. I rarely see this kick outside the realm of Muay Thai, where it's used often. This kick is not only powerful; once you learn the footwork and the pivot you'll be surprised how fast you can throw this kick. You can increase the odds of landing the second kick to your opponent's head by either throwing a jab-right cross-single switch step kick to his body as a set-up, or by attacking his body with back kicks. Either of these versions executed a couple of times should enable you to go to your opponent's head with the second kick with favorable results.

DOUBLE JAB-WHIPPING ROUND KICK

A slight variation of an earlier technique, a double-jab-whipping round kick with the rear leg is one of the simplest, yet most brutally effective

combinations you can use. This one has a single purpose: To knock your opponent out and end the fight. The two jabs distract your opponent and back him up, giving you the necessary room for the high kick.

Although your jabs may cause your opponent to raise his arms to cover his head and face, with this kick it really

doesn't matter. Even if he blocks it, the height, power, trajectory of the kick and the weight of your leg will most likely blast your kick through his guard. And if your opponent manages to get his head out of the way of your kick, you'll still knock his arms down, leaving his head wide open to attack from your punches.

As I said earlier, the momentum of this kick is so great that if you miss, you'll spin back to your original position. This can be used to your advantage, as you could conceivably kick, miss, spin around and throw the same kick again, in hopes of catching an opponent who was closing in on you to counter. This kick is a finishing technique, and you must throw it like you mean business.

While these are my favorite combinations, the beauty of kickboxing is that it allows you to take the basic techniques we discussed in both boxing and kicking, and combine them in a way is uniquely your own. This is where the kickboxer becomes the artist, which is one of the main attractions the sport holds for me. Practice these techniques, but don't be afraid to improvise on them, using the techniques that work best for you. After all, you're the one putting in the work, it ought to be fun.

SECTION V

WRAPPING IT UP

PARTING SHOTS

So you're a dragon, now what?

Well, you've studied your attacking techniques, your defensive techniques and your countering techniques, so now you're a kickboxing expert, right? Wrong. You now have exactly enough information to be dangerous, to yourself and to others. Learning technique and mastering technique are as different as crawling and running. What comes now is practice, practice and more practice. That's how the crawler becomes the runner.

Kickboxing is an exciting sport, great aerobic exercise and a killer method of self-defense, but if you're going to get into it, you've got to be dedicated. People always say, "You get out of something what you put into it." But I don't think that applies to kickboxing. I think you have to put more into it just to get a little out. You have to work hard. It seems like you've got to climb a mountain just to throw one punch. If you miss climbing that mountain, or think about missing climbing that mountain, the punch wavers. "Hey, I'm going to do it tomorrow," won't cut it.

You must be dedicated. You can't be soft, and devote time to it every now and then. To master a technique, you need to build upon your continual training, each session adding a little bit to your skill level, like climbing that mountain, one step at a time. If you miss a session or two, you'll find you're back to a lower level, and will need to take the same steps over again. It's easier, and more productive, to only have to take those steps once, and you'll be amazed by your progress.

But you can't take your training lightly. You could hurt yourself if you're not serious enough, or worse, you could hurt someone else. And there's no reason a training partner should have to pay for your mistakes.

You don't have to be Mr. or Ms. Dead Serious all of the time, but you need to be responsible. The idea is to have fun, but don't get careless. Accidents can be forever.

Don't just focus on the punches and kicks, either. Yes, they're the fun part. But we arranged the lessons in the order they appear for a reason. Stay in shape. I run every day. Always do your warm ups, and do them well. I've skimped on the stretches before, and paid the price of a pulled hamstring. Your stretches reduce injuries, period. Try some of these moves cold and you'll quickly find out how important they are.

When practicing these punches and kicks, focus on mastering the technique. Strength is important, sure, but when two fighters of equal size and conditioning, one a little stronger and the other better technically, meet, put your money on the technician. Now if the strong guy masters technique, you've got trouble. Good technique shows you've taken pride in yourself and your art.

There's no way your combinations will be effective if your technique is bad, since combinations build on the previous punch or kick. Yours will only get worse with each move, unless you've taken the effort to master each technique. And if you're throwing good, crisp punches and solid kicks, your combos will feel great—to you anyway, your opponent may not agree. Lastly, your counters will be nasty when you're firing on all cylinders. Take the time, do the work, and before you know it you'll be one powerful fighting machine.

But with that power comes responsibility. If you're training for the ring, use that power in the ring. If you're looking to get in shape or defend yourself on the street, use it only when you have to. There is no justification for a trained kickboxer, or fighter of any kind, to go looking for trouble. You may be tempted to show off your new toy, but you must rise above the urge. Yeah, maybe the guy was a jerk and maybe he thought he was tough, but is that reason enough to reel off a jab-round kick-overhand elbow-knee combo and send him off to the emergency room?

The mugger deserves no mercy. Do what you must to get away safely. When you're in the ring, you fight to win. Do your best, and stay within the rules. Real life is full of jerks and fools "who've got it coming," but it's not your place to give it to them. Just because you can, doesn't mean you should. You can try to justify crossing the line all you want, but inside you'll know the truth.

Truth is in mastering yourself, your body and your mind. Truth is when you look across at your opponent and he looks like he's been eating nails and spitting rust, but you suck it up and go beyond that. You stay calm and stay controlled and go work your art. You are a martial artist, a fighter, not a bully.

This may be a hard temptation to resist for some of the more hard-core fighters among you, because sometimes that's part of what drives someone to be a professional fighter. Benny "the Jet" Urquidez once told me, "Some fighters fight because they want to put on a show. Some guys fight because they like hurting people." Put me in that first group. If you're part of that second bunch, chill out.

Sensei Bob once asked me, "Why do you fight?"

I said, "Well, because I train very hard and I'm kind of good at it." I wanted to be polite. This was in the days when a sensei could kick your butt if he wanted to.

"Nope."

"Because I train hard and I'm very good at it?"

"Cocky....Nope. Because we want you to. Me, your mom, your sisters, your friends, your buddies. We want you to, and we respect you. How do your teachers treat you? You can get away with stuff the other kids can't do, right?"

He was right, as usual. I got respect and was treated well by everyone because I was a fighter, and that was cool. But mostly because I was a good fighter, and did the work it took to be my best. When you work hard, and give it your best shot, people respect you, whether you're fighting or baking cookies.

But to be respected, you must deserve respect. A friend of mine, an amateur fighter, told me that when he spars with Hector Lopez or me, we're pretty cool with him. But some of the other pros, they want to give him some. They need to prove who's in charge. This isn't necessary for pros, and it's not necessary when you're sparring or working out with a partner.

Show some respect. You're both there to learn and train, and you won't prove yourself to be the better person by giving him unnecessary shots. Just the opposite. If you run into a partner who decides to play the big man and give it to you, crack him back. Give what you get. If it starts to get out of hand, walk away. If you can't work it out with your partner, talk to your instructor in private.

I keep an eye open for these types in my classes, and take them aside for a little talk.

"Joey. Joey. Joey. JOEY! Head 'em up, Joey. Okay Joey, check this out. Now, this guy doesn't want to spar with you any more. And the guys over there don't want to spar with you either. Neither does anyone else, including me. Now what?"

Sometimes I have to tell them 10 times a day, in that one class, lighter, lighter, lighter. There's usually one, maybe two guys in a class I have to tell that. These are the guys you want to avoid as a student; they'll crack you. And try to explain that black eye back at the office tomorrow.

At the same time, those of you who are going to be hard-core fighters want the Joeys to work with, to get you used to the contact. You'll meet some mean guys along the way, but if you want to fight, you handle it.

The training path before you is wide open; you need to decide what you want and what drives you. For me, there was a child's dream to be like Bruce Lee, and be that martial arts hero. Whenever I take anything on, I always seem to take the roughest one. I always strive for a seemingly impossible goal or dream and then I go for it. I need something to put my all into, or I'd be restless. I've achieved my dream, for now.

But there are some very good fighters out there, and there will always be another kid. It could be a Thailander, a Japanese, or anybody. It's always somebody new, but I'm still the man. It's that ego thing with athletes. Someone says, "There's a new kid, man, and he's gonna whup Petey!" It's a challenge. You have to rise, and say, "Here we go again." You've got to prove it.

I'm always trying to improve. I never want to hear someone say, "Oh, man, you fought better the last time." That would hurt. Every time out, I want people to say, "That was his best fight."

I have to live with myself, and I'm my harshest critic. I always want to win, but I'll never be one of those guys who gets taken out of the ring on a stretcher while his opponent stands there without a scratch, but the judges give him the decision. "Hey, I won. The judge says I won, so I won." That's not me. If I ever get beat (and don't bet on this), I'll be man enough to acknowledge it.

If the judges give me a fight I believe I lost, I'll take the mike.

"This evening I was bested by this gentleman. Sir, you are now the champ." I'd give him the belt and walk out. What are they going to do? They can't call be back, I'm already gone. They'd probably be mad, with egg all over their faces, but what, they're going to suspend me? I'd quit anyway. Get out of my face. He's the man now.

But it won't happen. When I step into the ring, I'm going to do what I'm going to do. I'm not going to wait for my opponent to make his move. I'm the ring general, I dictate. Maybe the guy moves too good and is determined to take the first shot. Fine, but if I can't muss this kid, I'll slick

him. That's one thing that's forever— the tricks of the trade. Spinning, little tricks, whatever it takes to put him out. There's no substitute for experience. And experience only comes with time, and practice.

So now it's your turn. Take these techniques and practice, practice and practice until you make them your own, and then practice them some more. Have some fun with it, but never lose your focus. Your confidence will build as your skill rises. Your body will look better than you thought it could. Mom, you can carry your groceries in with confidence. And the dragons? I'll see *you* in the ring.

ACKNOWLEDGEMENTS

Sugarfoot would like to thank...
Tom "Yosemite Sam" Forstreuter and Doug Dunn, my "big brothers," for discovering me and always having faith and confidence in me. Bob Supeene, Jr., for putting the heart of a warrior in me, and for teaching me how to be a winner; Edward "Pops" Couzens for working me hard when I needed it, for showing me the importance of honor and self-respect, and for teaching me how *not* to be like others, but to set an example instead; Ray Barnes for one of the best lessons I've ever learned: "All the world loves a winner, but as soon as you lose, they're gone. Remember that when you step in the ring." I have.
...and Mom and my sisters, the loves of my life.

Snake would like to thank...
Unk, for *always* being there; Mom and Dad, for letting me find my own path; Big Brother and the Bug for love and support; Petey, Don "The Foot" and Chris "The Lad" for presenting the sword, what a team!; Greg and Lisa at Galt for service above and beyond; Rui, for agreeing to this project and first class assistance thereof; Atilla the Hun Club, for setting the wheels in motion; Dale and the Bandit for standing up with me; Chas (and Chips the mascot) at KO Arts for pugilistic tutelage without peer; my warrior brothers and sisters from the Judo & Karate Academy of Colorado Springs, 1981-85, those truly were the good old days.
...and a special thank-you to Sensei John Saylor and Sensei Dan Pyhtila, my judo instructors, for showing me by example what it means to be a warrior. I have not forgotten.

PETER CUNNINGHAM is a legendary figure in the martial arts community. Rated by experts as one of the greatest full-contact fighters of all time, Cunningham is an undefeated six-time world champion kickboxer. Belts Cunningham has won include the World Karate Association Lightweight Title, the WKA Superlightweight Title and the WKA Junior Welter Weight Title. As of 1995 he holds the Karate International Council of Kickboxing Super Lightweight Title and the International Muay Thai Federation Junior Welter Weight Title.

The charismatic Cunningham now turns his attention toward the film world. Soon audiences worldwide will see Cunningham's unsurpassed fighting skill and talent on the big screen. Peter Cunningham is the *real* action star of the '90s.

ROBERT MICKEY started his martial arts training in Colorado in 1978, where he earned a black belt in karate and a brown belt in judo. His eloquent teaching style and focus on realistic training and self-defense earned the respect of his students, while his elusive fighting style against larger opponents did the same with his fellow instructors. He started training in kickboxing under Peter Cunningham in 1989 at the world famous Jet Center in Van Nuys, California, where he eventually served as Cunningham's assistant instructor. Mr. Mickey lives in Orange County, California with his wife Kim, and he hopes that someday Cunningham will forgive him for cutting off his "Conan" hair.